Cambridge English

Complete IELTS

Bands 5–6.5

Workbook *without Answers*

Mark Harrison

CAMBRIDGE
UNIVERSITY PRESS

CAMBRIDGE
UNIVERSITY PRESS & ASSESSMENT

Shaftesbury Road, Cambridge CB2 8EA, United Kingdom

One Liberty Plaza, 20th Floor, New York, NY 10006, USA

477 Williamstown Road, Port Melbourne, VIC 3207, Australia

314–321, 3rd Floor, Plot 3, Splendor Forum, Jasola District Centre, New Delhi – 110025, India

103 Penang Road, #05–06/07, Visioncrest Commercial, Singapore 238467

Cambridge University Press & Assessment is a department of the University of Cambridge.

We share the University's mission to contribute to society through the pursuit of
education, learning and research at the highest international levels of excellence.

www.cambridge.org
Information on this title: www.cambridge.org/9781009672177

© Cambridge University Press & Assessment 2012

First published 2012
20 19 18 17 16 15 14 13 12 11 10 9 8 7 6 5 4 3 2 1

Printed in Great Britain by Ashford Colour Limited

A catalogue record for this publication is available from the British Library

ISBN 978-1-009-68364-7 Student's Book with Answers
ISBN 978-1-009-68363-0 Student's Book without Answers
ISBN 978-0-521-18516-5 Teacher's Book
ISBN 978-1-009-67218-4 Workbook with Answers
ISBN 978-1-009-67217-7 Workbook without Answers

Additional resources for this publication at www.cambridge.org/elt/workbookwithoutanswers

Contents

Map of the units   4

1   **Starting somewhere new**   6

2   **It's good for you!**   12

3   **Getting the message across**   18

4   **New media**   24

5   **The world in our hands**   30

6   **Making money, spending money**   36

7   **Relationships**   42

8   **Fashion and design**   48

Recording script   54

Acknowledgements   61

Map of the units

Unit title	Reading	Listening
1 Starting somewhere new	Reading Section 1: *Third culture kids* • True / False / Not given • Table completion	Listening Part 1: Conducting a survey • Form completion • Multiple choice
2 It's good for you!	Reading Section 2: *What do you know about the food you eat?* • Matching headings • Pick from a list	Listening Part 2: A welcome talk • Multiple choice • Labelling a map or a plan
3 Getting the message across	Reading Section 3: *Strictly English* • Yes / No / Not given • Summary completion with a box • Multiple choice	Listening Part 3: A student tutorial • Pick from a list • Matching • Short-answer questions
4 New media	Reading Section 1: *Is constant use of electronic media changing our minds?* • True / False / Not given • Note completion • Short-answer questions	Listening Part 4: A talk on blogging • Sentence completion • Flow-chart completion
5 The world in our hands	Reading Section 2: *Russia's boreal forests and wild grasses could combat climate change* • Matching information • Matching features • Summary completion	Listening Part 1: Finding out about environmental projects • Note completion • Table completion
6 Making money, spending money	Reading Section 1: *Movers and shakers* • Labelling a diagram • True / False / Not given • Flow-chart completion	Listening Part 2: A talk about vending machines • Matching • Labelling a diagram
7 Relationships	Reading Section 2: *Establishing your birthrights* • Matching headings • Matching features • Sentence completion	Listening Part 3: A student discussion about a presentation • Multiple choice • Flow-chart completion
8 Fashion and design	Reading Section 3: *Making a loss is the height of fashion* • Multiple choice • Yes / No / Not given • Matching sentence endings	Listening Part 4: A lecture on the history of jeans • Sentence completion

Writing	Vocabulary	Grammar
Writing Task 1 • Selecting important information • Planning an answer	• *Problem* or *trouble*? • *Affect* or *effect*? • *Percent* or *percentage* • Key vocabulary	Making comparisons
Writing Task 2: A task with two questions • Analysing the task • Organising ideas into paragraphs • Using linking words	• Word formation • Key vocabulary	Countable and uncountable nouns
Writing Task 1 • Summarising trends in graphs and tables	• *Teach*, *learn* or *study*? • *Find out* or *know*? • Study-related vocabulary • Key vocabulary	• Tenses: past simple, present perfect simple and present perfect continuous • Prepositions in time phrases and phrases describing trends
Writing Task 2: To what extent do you agree or disagree? • Answering the question • Choosing relevant information • Using linkers	• *Cause, factor* and *reason* • Internet-related vocabulary • Key vocabulary	• *However, although, even though* and *on the other hand* • Articles
Writing Task 1 • Summarising a diagram • Analysing the task • Writing in paragraphs • Ordering information • Using sequencers	• *Nature, the environment* or *the countryside*? • *Tourist* or *tourism*? • Key vocabulary	The passive
Writing Task 2: Agreeing and disagreeing • Introducing and linking ideas in paragraphs • Constructing the middle paragraphs of an essay	• Verb + *to do* / verb + *doing* • Words connected with finance • Words connected with shops and shopping • Key vocabulary	Relative pronouns and relative clauses
Writing Task 1 • Analysing similarities and differences in charts / graphs • Using reference devices	• Words related to feelings and attitudes • *Age(s)* / *aged* / *age group* • Key vocabulary	• Reference devices • Zero, first and second conditionals
Writing Task 2: Discussing two opinions • Including your own opinion • Introducing other people's opinions • Concluding paragraphs	• *Dress* (uncountable) / *dress* (*es*) (countable) / *clothes* / *cloth* • Key vocabulary	Time conjunctions: *until* / *before* / *when* / *after*

Starting somewhere new

Listening Part 1

❶ **Look at the second task, Question 6–10. What do all of the questions focus on? Circle A, B or C.**

A how often the man does various things
B a particular aspect of life in the city
C planned changes in the city

❷ (02) **Now listen and answer Questions 1–10.**

Questions 1–5

Complete the form below.

*Write **NO MORE THAN TWO WORDS AND/OR A NUMBER** for each answer.*

INTERVIEW – DETAILS OF SUBJECT	
Age group:	..25-34..
Length of time living in city:	1 ....
Previous home:	2 ....
Occupation:	3 ....
Area of city:	4 ....
Postcode:	5 ....

Questions 6–10

*Choose the correct letter, **A**, **B** or **C**.*

6 What does the man say about public transport?

A He doesn't like using it.
B He seldom uses it.
C He has stopped using it.

7 What does the man say about sport in the city?

A Some facilities are better than others.
B He intends to do more of it in the future.
C Someone recommended a place to him before he came.

8 What does the man say about entertainment?

A He doesn't have much time for it.
B There is a very wide range of it.
C It is the best aspect of life in the city.

9 What does the man say about litter?

A There is less of it than he had expected.
B Not enough is done about the problem.
C His home town has more of it.

10 What does the man say about crime in the city?

A The police deal with it very efficiently.
B It is something that worries him.
C He doesn't know how much of it there is.

Vocabulary

Problem or *trouble*?

❶ Complete these questions with *problem* or *trouble*.

1 What has been the main .... you have had in adapting to a new country?

2 Have you had .... communicating with people?

3 If you have a .... have you got someone who will help you?

4 Have you got into .... because of something you didn't understand?

5 Is the language a .... for you?

Affect or *effect*?

❷ Complete these questions with the correct form of *affect* or *effect*.

1 Have the people you've met had an .... on you?

2 Does the weather .... how you feel?

3 Has being away from your friends and family .... you more than you expected?

4 What have been the main .... of living in a new country?

5 What .... you the most – the people or the place?

Percent or *percentage*

▶ Student's Book unit 1, p15

❸ Complete these sentences about emigration from a country with *percent* or *percentage*.

1 The .....percentage... of people planning to emigrate rose last year.

2 Only a small .... planned to live abroad permanently.

3 The .... planning short-term emigration was higher last year than this year.

4 There was a rise of three .... in the number of people planning to leave.

5 Last year, four .... of people said that they were thinking of emigrating.

6 This year, 73 .... of people emigrating did so for reasons of employment.

Key vocabulary

❹ Complete the sentences below with the words in the box. There are two words which do not fit into any of the gaps.

accustomed	adjusting	customs	seek
~~surroundings~~	values	process	matters
sense	referring	evidence	stages

Moving to a new country

- Being in unfamiliar (1) ..surroundings.. can make you feel lonely.

- (2) .... to a new life is a difficult (3) .... You probably go through several (4) .... before you start to feel comfortable.

- It can be hard to understand how to deal with financial (5) .... because the system is so different from the one you are (6) .... to.

- Researchers have found (7) .... that certain personality types have less trouble than others in getting used to living abroad.

- If some of the (8) .... in your new country don't make (9) .... to you, it's a good idea to (10) .... out people from your own culture who can explain them to you.

Reading Section 1

❶ Read the title and the first three paragraphs of the article below. Who are 'Third culture kids'? Circle A, B or C.

A children whose parents keep moving from country to country

B children living in a country neither of their parents come from

C children who have just arrived in a culture that is new to them

❷ Now read the whole text and answer Questions 1–13.

THIRD CULTURE KIDS

In a world where international careers are becoming commonplace, the phenomenon of third culture kids (TCKs) – children who spend a significant portion of their developmental years in a culture outside their parents' passport culture(s) – is increasing exponentially. Not only is their number increasing, but the cultural complexity and relevance of their experience and the adult TCKs (ATCKs) they become, is also growing.

When Ruth Hill Useem, a sociologist, first coined this term in the 1950s, she spent a year researching expatriates in India. She discovered that folks who came from their home (or first) culture and moved to a host (or second) culture, had, in reality, formed a culture, or lifestyle, different from either the first or second cultures. She called this the third culture and the children who grew up in this lifestyle 'third culture kids'. At that time, most expatriate families had parents from the same culture and they often remained in one host culture while overseas.

This is no longer the case. Take, for example, Brice Royer, the founder of TCKid.com. His father is a half-French/half-Vietnamese UN peacekeeper, while his mom is Ethiopian. Brice lived in seven countries before he was eighteen including France, Mayotte, La Réunion, Ethiopia, Egypt, Canada and England. He writes, 'When people ask me "Where are you from?" I just joke around and say, "My mom says I'm from heaven." ' What other answer can he give?

ATCK Elizabeth Dunbar's father, Roy, moved from Jamaica to Britain as a young boy. Her mother, Hortense, was born in Britain as the child of Jamaican immigrants who always planned to repatriate 'one day'. While Elizabeth began life in Britain, her dad's international career took the family to the United States, then to Venezuela and back to living in three different cities in the U.S. She soon realised that while racial diversity may be recognised, the hidden cultural diversity of her life remained invisible.

Despite such complexities, however, most ATCKs say their experience of growing up among different cultural worlds has given them many priceless gifts. They have seen the world and often learnt several languages. More importantly, through friendships that cross the usual racial, national or social barriers, they have also learned the very different ways people see life. This offers a great opportunity to become social and cultural bridges between worlds that traditionally would never connect. ATCK Mikel Jentzsch, author of a best-selling book in Germany, *Bloodbrothers – Our Friendship*

in Liberia, has a German passport but grew up in Niger and then Liberia. Before the Liberian civil war forced his family to leave, Mikel played daily with those who were later forced to become soldiers for that war. Through his eyes, the stories of those we would otherwise overlook come to life for the rest of us.

Understanding the TCK experience is also important for other reasons. Many ATCKs are now in positions of influence and power. Their capacity to often think 'outside the box' can offer new and creative thinking for doing business and living in our globalising world. But that same thinking can create fear for those who see the world from a more traditional world view. Neither the non-ATCKs nor the ATCKs may recognise that there may be a cultural clash going on because, by traditional measures of diversity such as race or gender, they are alike.

In addition, many people hear the benefits and challenges of the TCK profile described and wonder why they relate to it when they never lived overseas because of a parent's career. Usually, however, they have grown up cross-culturally in another way, perhaps as children of immigrants, refugees, bi-racial or bi-cultural unions, international adoptees, even children of minorities. If we see the TCK experience as a Petri dish of sorts – a place where the effects of growing up among many cultural worlds accompanied by a high degree of mobility have been studied – then we can look for what lessons may also be relevant to helping us understand issues other cross-cultural kids (CCKs) may also face. It is possible we may discover that we need to rethink our traditional ways of defining diversity and identity. For some, as for TCKs, 'culture' may be something defined by shared experience rather than shared nationality or ethnicity. In telling their stories and developing new models for our changing world, many will be able to recognise and use well the great gifts of a cross-cultural childhood and deal successfully with the challenges for their personal, communal and corporate good.

Questions 1–6

Do the following statements agree with the information given in the reading passage?

Write

TRUE　　　　if the statement agrees with the information

FALSE　　　if the statement contradicts the information

NOT GIVEN　if there is no information on this

1　There is a close connection between careers and the number of TCKs.

2　An increasing number of people describe themselves as TCKs.

3　Ruth Hill Useem studied children in several countries.

4　Ruth Hill Useem defined the third culture as a mixture of two parents' original cultures.

5　Brice Royer feels that he has benefited greatly from living in many different countries.

6　Elizabeth Dunbar felt that she had a culture that was different from most people's.

Questions 7–13

Complete the table below.

Choose **NO MORE THAN THREE WORDS** from the passage for each answer.

THIRD CULTURE KIDS – ADVANTAGES AND RESULTS		
Area	**Advantage for ATCKs**	**Possible result**
Friendships	know how different people 7	can act as bridges between worlds that are usually separate
Business	creative thinking	may cause 8 .... among certain people can lead to 9 .... despite similarities
Whole experience	knowledge of many cultural worlds and a great deal of 10	can teach us about problems faced by 11 .... of all kinds current ideas of what both 12 .... mean may be considered wrong belief that culture depends on 13 ....

Writing Task 1

1 Look at the chart below. Which of the descriptions, A–C, correctly matches the chart? Why are the other descriptions not appropriate?

A The chart below shows levels of emigration from Bulgaria in the 15–60 age group in 2001 and 2006.

B The chart below shows the plans of Bulgarian people aged 15–60 concerning leaving Bulgaria and living or working in another country in 2001 and 2006.

C The chart below compares reasons why Bulgarians aged 15–60 decided to leave Bulgaria in 2001 and 2006.

Emigration intentions, Bulgarians aged 15–60, 2001 & 2006

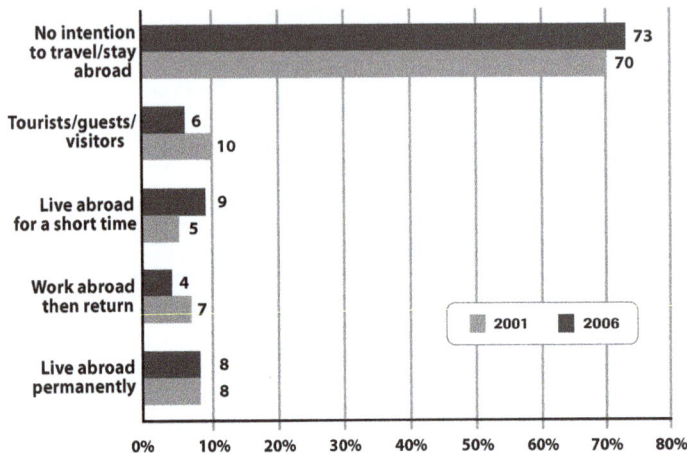

2 Answer these questions about the chart.

1 What did most Bulgarians aged 15–60 plan to do in both years? ....

2 Which categories were higher in 2006 than in 2001? ....

3 What was the lowest category in 2001? ....

4 What happened in the category of people intending to live abroad permanently? ....

5 Which categories were higher in 2001 than in 2006? ....

3 Look at this Writing task and decide which of the statements below are correct or not. Write *Yes* or *No*.

The chart below gives information about the level of education of Bulgarian people who wanted to go and live in another country in 2002, 2006 and 2008.

Summarise the information by selecting and reporting the main features, and make comparisons where relevant.

Level of education of Bulgarians planning to leave Bulgaria

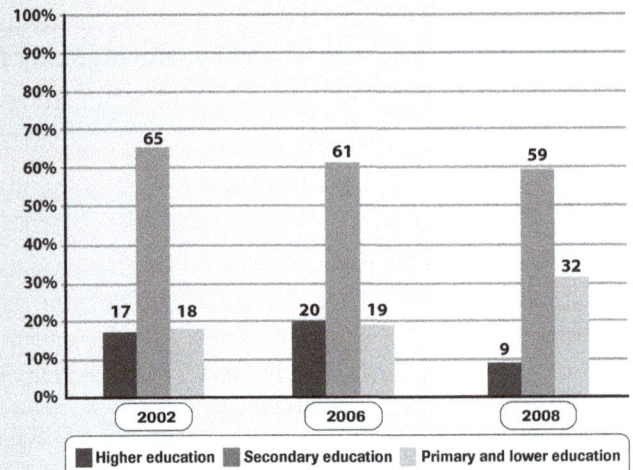

1 The figure for people with higher education level fell in both 2006 and 2008. ....

2 One of the categories was the highest in every year. ....

3 Two of the categories rose in 2006. ....

4 One of the categories was lower in 2008 than in 2002. ....

5 The figure for people with primary and lower education rose each year. ....

6 The figure for secondary education was a lot lower in 2008 than in 2006. ....

4 Now write your answer for the Writing task in Exercise 3.

Grammar

Making comparisons

❶ This email is from Krishna, who has gone to live abroad. Complete the sentences with the comparative or superlative form of the adjective or adverb in brackets.

✉

Hi Neha,

Well, I've been here for a month now and things are fine. Of course, everything here is different from what I'm used to, and I'm finding some things (1) ....*easier*......... (easy) to deal with than others.

The course is (2) .... (demanding) than I expected and I'm having to work (3) .... (hard) than I ever have before. (4) .... (difficult) aspect of the course is the amount of work we have to do. Last week I had to write five essays – that's (5) .... (tiring) thing I've ever done! The best aspect of the course is the other students. They're (6) .... (friendly) people I've ever met and because of them I'm (7) .... (stressed) now than I was the first week of the course.

Lots of things have changed for me in comparison with my life at home. I have to travel (8) .... (far) to college, a lot of things are (9) .... (expensive) and the weather is a lot (10) .... (bad)! The city is (11) .... (big) than anywhere I've lived before and life is (12) .... (fast) here. I've never been (13) .... (busy) than I am now but this is (14) .... (exciting) thing I've ever done and I'm really pleased that I'm here!

I'll write to you (15) .... (regular) in future.

Love,

Krishna

❷ Complete the first sentence with the comparative or superlative form of the word in brackets. Then complete the second sentence so that it has a similar meaning to the first sentence.

1 a The town I come from is a lot ....*smaller*.... (small) than this one.

   b This town is .....*bigger*...... than the one I come from.

2 a Money is a problem because life here is .... (expensive) than life at home.

   b Money is a problem because life at home is .... than life here.

3 a I am .... (old) person in my class.

   b The other people in my class are .... than me.

4 a The transport system here is .... (good) than the one at home.

   b The transport system at home is .... than the one here.

5 a People here speak .... (slow) than people at home.

   b People at home speak .... than people here.

6 a Moving to another country is .... (difficult) thing you can do!

   b Nothing is .... than moving to another country.

Unit 2   It's good for you!

Reading   Section 2

❶ **Read through the article briefly. What does it mainly contain? Circle A, B or C.**

   A   advice on healthy eating

   B   facts about food and drink

   C   criticism of the food industry

❷ **Now read the text carefully and answer Questions 1–13.**

WHAT DO YOU KNOW ABOUT THE FOOD YOU EAT?

A   Most of us tend not to think about what we eat. Sure, we might have our favourite recipes, or worry about whether our food has been sprayed with pesticides, but the processes and discoveries that have gone into its production remain a closed book. Some, however, think differently. Why, they wonder, is frozen milk yellow? Why does your mouth burn for longer when you eat chillies than when you eat mustard? And what would happen if you threw yourself into a swimming pool full of jelly?

B   It was for such people that *New Scientist* developed its 'Last Word' column, in which readers pose – and answer – questions on all manner of abstruse scientific issues, as they relate to everyday life. Many of the issues raised have simple answers. For the questions above, they would be: the riboflavin in milk begins to crystallise; it depends on your taste – the relevant chemical in mustard is more easily washed away by your saliva; and, you'd float, but don't dive in headfirst!

C   Other questions allow us to explore issues that are relevant to everyone. For example, what's the difference between sell-by dates and use-by dates? You might expect the answer to involve overcautious health and safety regulation. But it's more complex than that. The shelf life of food is actually determined by its manufacturers, although lab tests and government guidelines also come into play. Food is tested periodically, at various temperatures, to check the level of bacterial spoilage over a few hours or days – the warmer it is, the more likely your prawn sandwich is to make you ill. After the lab tests, producers set a use-by date or a best-before date. Fresh shellfish need to be consumed by their use-by date (the date by which you must eat them). But tinned beans will probably last long beyond their best-before date (the date by which it's best to eat them), although they might not taste as good as they once did.

D   The same research explains why even bottled mineral water, which had previously lain underground for decades, needs a best-before date. The problem isn't the water, but the bottling process: either bacteria can be introduced that multiply and, over time, contaminate the water, or unpleasant chemicals, such as antimony, leach into the water from the plastic bottles.

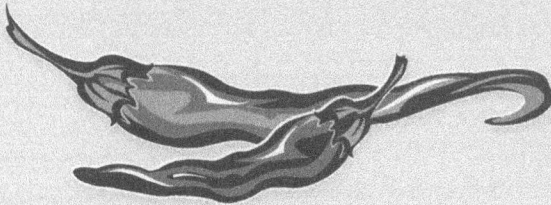

E Sometimes, this kind of scientific study takes us to some strange places. For example, we now know that the amount of oxygen in the air inside green peppers is higher than in red (by a whopping 1.23 percent), probably due to the different rate at which green peppers photosynthesise. The relevance of this research is that green peppers will decay faster than red if kept in sunlight: higher oxygen levels provide more resources to feed any bacteria that are present. Generally, cooler environments preserve food best – apart from tropical fruit. Banana skins, for example, have evolved to survive in warm conditions, because that is where they grow best. Anything below 13.3°C damages the membranes, releasing enzymes which lead to skin blackening. To avoid a mushy banana, keep it away from the chiller.

F It is not just fears for our health that keep food scientists busy. They are also involved in other areas. Their precision has, for example, also been applied to bottles – in particular, to the discovery that the optimum number of sharp pointy bits on a bottle cap is 21. Go on, count them. Years of trial and error led to the internationally accepted German standard DIN 6099, which ensures that almost every bottle cap is the same. This is because 21 is the ideal number when you take into account the circumference of the cap, the likelihood of its metal splitting, and the chances of it sticking in the capping machine. So, next time you open a bottle with a cap on it, pay homage to those who bothered to find out, starting with William Painter, in 1892.

G Of course, some researchers do care about the more serious stuff, driven by fear of the future and an ever-increasing population on a warming, land-impoverished planet. Sadly, *New Scientist*'s correspondents concluded that there was no one foodstuff that could feed the world on its own. However, they did come up with a menu that could feed a family of four for 365 days a year, using only eight square metres of land. Rotating crops (so that the soil didn't lose one nutrient more than any other) would be vital, as would ploughing back dead plant matter and maintaining a vegetarian diet. After that, you would need to grow crops that take up very little space and grow vertically rather than horizontally, if possible.

Questions 1–7

The reading passage has seven paragraphs, **A–G**.

*Choose the correct heading for paragraphs **A–G** from the list of headings below.*

i	Why a particular piece of information is given
ii	An unsolved problem and a solution to a problem
iii	Reasons that remain a mystery
iv	A source of information for some people
v	Development work leading to a conclusion
vi	Contrasting levels of interest in food
vii	The need to change a system
viii	Information connected with keeping certain kinds of food
ix	How certain advice is decided on
x	Ideas not put into practice

1 Paragraph A   ....vi....
2 Paragraph B   ....
3 Paragraph C   ....
4 Paragraph D   ....
5 Paragraph E   ....
6 Paragraph F   ....
7 Paragraph G   ....

Questions 8–13

*Choose **TWO** letters, **A–E**.*

Questions 8–9

*Which **TWO** of the following are explained by the writer in the text?*

A why the 'Last Word' column was created

B why use-by dates are more important than sell-by dates

C how to prevent bacteria getting into bottled water

D a way in which peppers are similar to bananas

E why most bottle caps have a common feature

Questions 10–11

*Which **TWO** problems connected with food does the writer mention?*

A confusing information about the use of pesticides

B feeling pain when eating something

C sell-by dates sometimes being inaccurate

D feeling ill because of eating food after its best-before date

E the effect of sunlight on green peppers

Questions 12–13

*Which **TWO** of the following would a family of four need to do to feed itself every day of the year, according to* New Scientist?

A use more than one piece of land

B grow the same crop all the time

C put dead plants into the soil

D plant only crops that grow very quickly

E concentrate on crops that grow vertically

Listening Part 2

❶ Look at both tasks. When is the speaker talking? Circle A, B or C.

A at the begining of a conference

B during the planning of a conference

C at the end of a conference

❷ (03) Now listen and answer Questions 1–10.

Questions 1–5

*Choose the correct letter, **A**, **B** or **C**.*

1 The speaker says that the conference includes issues which

  A were requested by participants.

  B are seldom discussed.

  C cause disagreement.

2 The speaker says that in the past, this subject

  A caused problems in the workplace.

  B was not something companies focused on.

  C did not need to be addressed.

3 The speaker mentions a connection between health and fitness and

  A keeping employees.

  B employees' performance.

  C a company's reputation.

4 What does the speaker say about the people attending the conference?

  A Some of them may feel that there is not much they can learn.

  B All of them have attended the conference before.

  C Most of them are familiar with the speakers.

5 The speaker says that in the sessions, participants will

  A work together in pairs.

  B pretend to have various roles.

  C describe real events.

Questions 6–10

Label the map below.

*Write the correct letter, **A–H**, next to questions 6–10.*

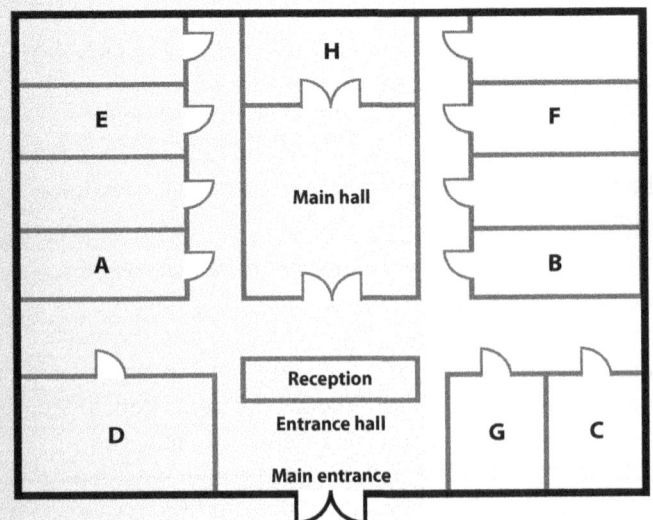

6 Setting Up a Fitness Centre ....

7 Healthy Eating Schemes ....

8 Transport Initiatives ....

9 Running Sports Teams ....

10 Conference Coordinator's Office ....

Vocabulary

Word formation

❶ Complete each sentence with the correct form of the word in brackets.

1 Healthy eating is a matter of ...*education*... so that people know what to eat. (educate)

2 Yesterday she .... him for being too lazy to keep fit. (critic)

3 Even if exercise is .... , it's better than no exercise. (regular)

4 Going for a run on a .... day is a nice way to spend your time. (sun)

5 .... exercise is essential for everyone. (day)

6 Sometimes children don't want to eat healthy food because of its .... (appear)

7 There is a connection between being healthy and having a high level of .... (happy).

8 People who are .... can have health problems that fitter people don't have. (active)

❷ Complete the second sentence so that it has a similar meaning to the first. Use the correct form of the <u>underlined</u> word in the first sentence.

1 a The manufacturers claim that the additives don't do children any <u>harm</u>.

   b The manufacturers claim that the additives are ...*harmless*... to children.

2 a There has been a <u>dramatic</u> rise in the number of obese people in this country.

   b The number of obese people in this country has risen ....

3 a Food producers should make the information on their products <u>simpler</u>.

   b Food producers should .... the information on their products.

4 a There were a lot of people <u>running</u> in the park.

   b There were a lot of .... in the park.

5 a I was <u>surprised</u> that I got fit so quickly.

   b It was .... to me that I got fit so quickly.

6 a There were some figures that people didn't <u>expect</u> in the report on the nation's health.

   b There were some .... figures in the report on the nation's health.

Key vocabulary

❸ Complete the sentences below, then use the words to complete this crossword.

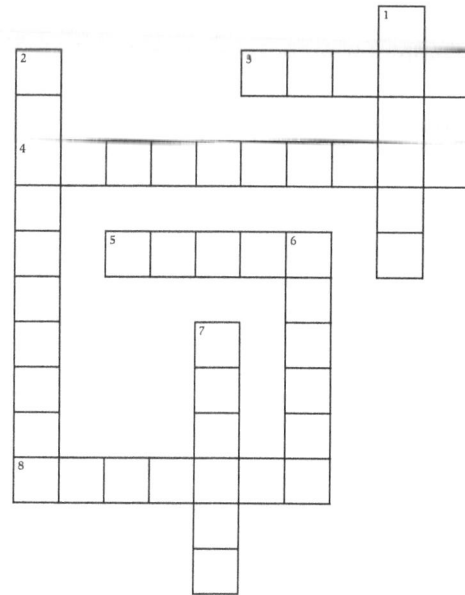

Across

3 Farmers who grow organic vegetables have to .... using pesticides.

4 Farming .... are the ways farming is done.

5 A food .... is a small structure where you can buy food, for example in a market or in a street.

8 If food is grown or produced .... , it comes from the area nearby.

Down

1 If something is .... to happen, it will probably happen.

2 If something is .... , it is not natural.

6 .... goods are high-quality, expensive goods.

7 Crop .... are the amount of crops produced in a particular place.

Writing Task 2

❶ Read the following Writing task.

> Write about the following topic:
>
> *Some people say that in the modern world it is very difficult for people to have a healthy lifestyle. Others, however, say that it is easy for people to be healthy and fit if they want to be.*
>
> *Discuss both these views and give your own opinion.*
>
> Give reasons for your answer and include any relevant examples from your knowledge or experience.

Below are three essay plans that candidates made for this question. Which one is the best essay plan for this question? Why is it the best one and why are the others not as good?

A

Paragraph 1:	introduce the issue: healthy/ unhealthy lifestyles
Paragraph 2:	why some people have unhealthy lifestyles
Paragraph 3:	more reasons for unhealthy and unfit people
Paragraph 4:	what people can do to be healthy and fit
Paragraph 5:	conclusion: it's easy to be healthy and fit

B

Paragraph 1:	introduction: why it's easy to have a healthy lifestyle
Paragraph 2:	what I do to stay fit and healthy
Paragraph 3:	some advice on healthy eating
Paragraph 4:	conclusion: anyone can be fit and healthy if they want to be

C

Paragraph 1:	introduce the subject: problem of unhealthy lifestyles
Paragraph 2:	reasons why some people have unhealthy lifestyles
Paragraph 3:	examples of unhealthy food and eating
Paragraph 4:	why some people aren't fit
Paragraph 5:	the results for people of having unhealthy lifestyles
Paragraph 6:	conclusion: it's a big problem

❷ Complete the phrases below, that could be used in the Writing task, with the verbs in the box.

| out | make | lose | take | ~~have~~ | stay |
| work | go | lead | do | | |

1 ......have......... health problems
2 .... a healthy life
3 .... fit
4 .... you good
5 .... out in a gym
6 .... action
7 .... down on unhealthy foods
8 .... an effort
9 .... on a diet
10 try to .... weight

❸ To write a good answer, you need to use linking words and phrases. Complete the sentences below with the words and phrases in the box.

| in fact | also | as a result | ~~over time~~ |
| another | in particular | on the other hand | |

1 If you exercise regularly, ...over time.... you will find that your general health improves.

2 People use their cars instead of walking. .... , they get very little exercise.

3 It is easy to buy healthy food in shops nowadays. .... , some of it is quite expensive.

4 Lack of exercise is one problem for some people. .... is the amount of junk food they eat.

5 There are gyms where people can get fit and there are .... ways of getting fit at home.

6 Some people think it's difficult to get fit. .... , it can be very easy.

7 Many people, ... office workers, have jobs that involve sitting in the same place all day.

❹ Now write your answer for the Writing task above.

Grammar

Countable and uncountable nouns

❶ Complete the sentences below with the plural or uncountable form of the words in the box.

group   research   job   way
knowledge   work   ~~programme~~
equipment   information   suggestion

1 More and more people nowadays are following fitness .programmes. .

2 It is easy to find .... on how to stay fit and healthy.

3 People with sedentary .... spend all day sitting down.

4 According to .... , the percentage of overweight people is growing.

5 This booklet contains many useful .... on how to keep fit.

6 Some people prefer to exercise in .... and so they join fitness classes.

7 At our gym, we have all the latest fitness .... for people to use.

8 Scientists are always increasing their .... of how the body works.

9 This book suggests a number of .... to help you lose weight.

10 My sister is looking for .... at a health centre as a receptionist.

❷ Circle the correct option in each of these sentences.

1 She does (plenty of) / much exercise and she's very fit.

2 There's a large / great deal of pollution in this city at this time of year.

3 It took me a lot of / many time to get fit again after my injury.

4 There is plenty / a wide range of fitness courses that you can do.

5 Bad diets cause a large amount / number of health problems.

6 Few / Little people these days think that fitness is unimportant.

7 A small amount / number of junk food isn't bad for you.

8 It doesn't take much / many effort to stay fit if you want to do it.

9 My grandfather is very lucky. He has few / a few problems with his health.

10 Even a few / a little exercise would be good for you.

❸ Correct the underlined nouns if necessary. Put a tick (✓) above the noun if it is correct.

1 People don't get much <u>informations</u> *[information]* on what is really in certain food <u>products</u> *[✓]*.

2 You don't need a large amount of <u>equipments</u> to do varied exercise <u>routines</u>.

3 People are given a lot of <u>advices</u> about how to have healthy <u>lifestyles</u>.

4 Junk food does a lot of <u>damages</u> to people's <u>healths</u>.

5 A nutritionist can give people good <u>advice</u> on their eating <u>habits</u>.

6 Using the latest <u>softwares</u>, experts analyse <u>sportsmen</u> when they are training.

7 People who do office <u>work</u> need to find <u>way</u> of keeping fit.

8 People sometimes need <u>help</u> to solve <u>problem</u> with their weight.

Listening Part 3

1 **Look at all of the tasks. What are the speakers talking about? Circle A, B or C.**

A a dissertation the student is planning

B a dissertation the student is writing

C a dissertation the student has completed

2 (04) **Now listen and answer Questions 1–10.**

Questions 1–4

*Choose **TWO** letters, A–E.*

Questions 1–2

*Which **TWO** areas of work did Beth include in her dissertation?*

A retail

B banking

C call centres

D tourism

E translation

Questions 3–4

*Which **TWO** aspects of the dissertation were impressive, according to the tutor?*

A summary of academic research

B analysis of videos

C observation of live interactions

D interviews

E analysis of data on the outcomes

Questions 5–8

Which comments do the speakers make about each section of the dissertation?

*Choose **FOUR** answers from the box and write the correct letter, A–F, next to Questions 5–8.*

Sections of Dissertation

5 Dealing with Complaints ....

6 Collaborating with Colleagues ....

7 Interacting with Managers ....

8 Giving Instructions ....

A There is not enough evidence.

B The conclusion is confusing.

C It highlights a real problem.

D It is particularly well organised.

E There are too many examples.

F It includes new ideas.

Questions 9–10

Answer the question below.

*Write **NO MORE THAN TWO WORDS** for each answer.*

*Which **TWO** aspects of communication does Beth emphasise in her conclusion?*

9 .... 10 ....

Vocabulary

▶ Student's Book unit 3, p28

❶ Complete this paragraph about a piece of college work with the words in the box. You may need to form a plural noun for some gaps.

evaluation	extract	weakness
finding	~~assignment~~	structure
assessment		feature

I've just done a big **(1)** *assignment* concerning language skills in various countries. To do this, I read short **(2)** .... from various long reports and I had to list the **(3)** .... of various research projects. I paid careful attention to the **(4)** .... of my report because it had to be well organised in clear sections. One of my **(5)** .... is that my work is sometimes not clear and well organised. When we've completed a piece of work, we are encouraged to do self- **(6)** .... to see if we find anything we can improve in our work, and then we have a system of peer **(7)** .... and comment on each other's work. One of the main **(8)** .... of my work is a comparison between the number of people who are literate and the number who can't read or write in various countries.

Teach, learn or *study*? *Find out* or *know*?

❷ Correct the underlined verbs if necessary. Put a tick (✓) above the verb if it is correct.

teach
1   Could you <u>learn</u> me how to change this picture on my computer?

2   Researchers have <u>found out</u> exactly why this happens.

3   I <u>learnt</u> a lot from doing that course.

4   I haven't been able to <u>know</u> much information on this topic.

5   I handed in my work last week but I don't <u>learn</u> what mark I got.

6   We had to <u>learn</u> hard because we had to write lots of essays.

7   If I <u>study</u> hard, I'm sure I'll do well.

8   Nobody <u>taught</u> me how to do this, I <u>found out</u> for myself.

Key vocabulary

❸ Complete the second sentences with one word so that they are similar in meaning to the first sentences.

1   How languages are learnt is an interesting subject.
    Language *acquisition* is an interesting subject.

2   English isn't his first language.
    He isn't a .... speaker of English.

3   It took me about five hours.
    It took me more or .... five hours.

4   This kind of work isn't easy for me.
    I don't .... this kind of work easy.

5   She doesn't belong to the Drama Club any more.
    She no .... belongs to the Drama Club.

6   I think he's trying to lose weight.
    I think he's on a ....

7   It's important to include statistical evidence in your work.
    The .... of statistical evidence in your work is important.

8   The important thing is that you get a good degree.
    What .... is that you get a good degree.

Reading Section 3

❶ Read through the article briefly and look at the second task, Questions 5–9.

In which paragraphs of the text will you find the information that you require to do this task?

....

❷ Now read the article carefully and answer Questions 1–14.

STRICTLY ENGLISH

British newspaper columnist Simon Heffer talks about his new book, 'Strictly English: the Correct Way to Write ... and Why It Matters', aimed at native speakers

For the last couple of years I have sent a round-robin email to my colleagues at this newspaper every few weeks pointing out to them mistakes that we make in our use of the English language. Happily, these are reasonably rare. The emails have been circulated on the Internet – and are now available on the paper's website – and one of them ended up in the inbox of a publisher at Random House about this time last year. He asked me whether I would write a book not just on what constituted correct English, but also why it matters. The former is relatively easy to do, once one has armed oneself with the *Oxford English Dictionary (OED)* and some reputable grammar books by way of research materials. The latter, being a matter for debate, is less straightforward.

I suppose my own interest in language started at school. Having studied French, Latin and Greek, I saw clearly how those languages had exported words into our own. When I studied German later on, I could see even more clearly why it was the sister tongue and what an enormous impact it had had on English. I saw that words had specific meanings and that, for the avoidance of doubt, it was best to use them in the correct way. Most of all, I became fascinated by grammar, and especially by the logic that drove it and that was common to all the other languages I knew. I did not intend in those days to earn a living by writing; but I was keen to ensure that my use of English was, as far as possible, correct.

Studying English at university forced me to focus even more intently on what words actually meant: why would a writer choose that noun rather than another and why that adjective – or, in George Orwell's case, often no adjective at all. Was the ambiguity in a certain order of words deliberate or accidental? The whole question of communication is rooted in such things. For the second part of my degree I specialised in the history of the English language, studying how words had changed their meaning and how grammar had evolved. Language had become not just a tool for me, but something of a hobby.

Can English, though, ever be fixed? Of course not: if you read a passage from Chaucer you will see that the meaning of words and the framework of grammar has shifted over the centuries, and both will continue to evolve. But we have had a standard dictionary now ever since the OED was completed in 1928, and learned men, many of whom contributed to the OED, wrote grammars a century ago that settled a pattern of language that was logical and free from the danger of ambiguity.

It is to these standards that I hope *Strictly English* is looking. Our language is to a great extent settled and codified, and to a standard that people recognise and are comfortable with. All my book does is describe and commend that standard, and help people towards a capable grasp of the English tongue. We shall always need new words to describe new things; but we don't need the wrong word to describe the right thing, when the right word exists. Also, English grammar shouldn't be a matter for debate. It has a coherent and logical structure and we should stick to it.

Some groups of people – state officials, academics, lawyers, certain breeds of scientist – talk to each other in a private language. Some official documents make little sense to lay people because they have to be written in a language that combines avoidance of the politically incorrect with constant use of the contemporary jargon of the profession. Some articles written by academics in particular are almost incomprehensible to those outside their circle. This is not because the outsiders are stupid. It is because the academics feel they have to write in a certain stilted, dense way in order to be taken seriously by their peers.

Many officials seem to have lost the knack of communicating with people outside their closed world.

Some academics, however, are bilingual. If asked to write for a publication outside the circle – such as a newspaper – they can rediscover the knack of writing reasonably plain English. They do not indulge themselves in such a fashion when they write for learned journals. It is almost as though the purpose of such writing is not to be clear: that the writer is recording research in order to prove to peers or superiors that he has discovered something. It does not seem to bother such people that their style is considered ugly and barbaric by anyone of discernment. It is repetitious, long-winded, abstract and abstruse. Those who write in such a way probably will not easily be discouraged, unless what is considered acceptable within their disciplines changes.

The ideal style is one comprehensible to any intelligent person. If you make a conscious decision to communicate with a select group, so be it: but in trying to appeal to a large audience, or even a small one that you wish to be sure will understand your meaning, writing of the sort mentioned above will not do. This sort of writing used to be kept from the general public thanks to the need to find someone to publish it. The advent of the Internet means that it is now much more widespread than it used to be; and the fact that it is now so common and so accessible means that this sort of writing is having a harmful effect on the language and causing it to be corrupted.

Questions 1–4

Do the following statements agree with the views of the writer in the reading passage?

Write

YES	*if the statement agrees with the views of the writer*
NO	*if the statement contradicts the views of the writer*
NOT GIVEN	*if it is impossible to say what the writer thinks about this*

1 The mistakes made by his colleagues are minor ones.

2 It is difficult to explain why using correct English is important.

3 English grammar has a different function from the grammar of other languages.

4 Word order may be as important as the choice of words used.

Questions 5–9

*Complete the summary using the list of words, **A–H**, below.*

The rules of English

According to the writer, the English language should not be considered something **5** ...., and this will always be the case. However, there have been accepted reference books for over a century that were produced by **6** .... people, and these have established a system for the language that enables people to express themselves in a completely clear way.

In his own book, the writer aims to describe and support the established rules of the language that are in **7** .... use and that people are accustomed to. He also wants his book to be **8** .... as a way of improving people's ability at the language. He believes that there is no reason why someone's use of vocabulary should not be correct and that grammar should not be a **9** .... subject. In his view, a system of grammar rules exists and people should always obey those rules.

A	simple	**E**	knowledgeable
B	general	**F**	compulsory
C	controversial	**G**	historic
D	permanent	**H**	useful

Questions 10–14

*Choose the correct letter, **A**, **B**, **C** or **D**.*

10 The writer says that some groups of people use a 'private language' because

A they do not want outsiders to be able to understand them.

B they want to show their superiority over other groups.

C they want to impress other members of their group.

D they do not want to use the same language as other groups.

11 According to the writer, some academics are capable of

A making sense to people outside their group.

B writing very clearly for learned journals.

C changing the way they communicate within their own group.

D explaining other people's work to the general public.

12 When discussing the writing of academics about their research, the writer emphasises

   A his own lack of knowledge of the academic world.

   B his desire to understand what they describe.

   C his sympathy for some of the academics.

   D his dislike for the style used in their writing.

13 The writer says that the kind of language used by academics in journals

   A is becoming more widely understood by non-academics.

   B is attracting a lot of criticism from other academics.

   C will only change if they are forced to change it.

   D appeals only to highly intelligent people.

14 The writer's opinion of the Internet is that

   A it is making people more aware of the poor use of language.

   B it is encouraging standards of language use to fall.

   C it is enabling people to compare good and poor use of language.

   D it is making it harder for good writing to get published.

Grammar

Tenses

❶ Complete these statements by IELTS candidates, using the past simple, present perfect or present perfect continuous forms of the verbs in the box. You may need to use a negative verb in some gaps.

have	~~get~~	find	write	put	give	be
work	look	make	study	leave		

1 I ....got......... a very good mark for my essay last week.

2 I'm very busy because my tutor .... me a very difficult piece of work to do.

3 I .... for a book on this subject for days but I .... one yet.

4 I .... this subject before, so I don't know much about it.

5 I .... on the student committee for two years but I .... it a few months ago because I .... enough time.

6 I .... on this project for three weeks and I'm making good progress.

7 I .... a few mistakes in the essay I .... yesterday.

8 I .... my name on the list for the college trip and I'm looking forward to it.

Prepositions

▶ Student's Book unit 3, p36

❷ Look at the graph from a communication company's report. Complete the sentences with the correct prepositions.

Mobile phone sales 2010

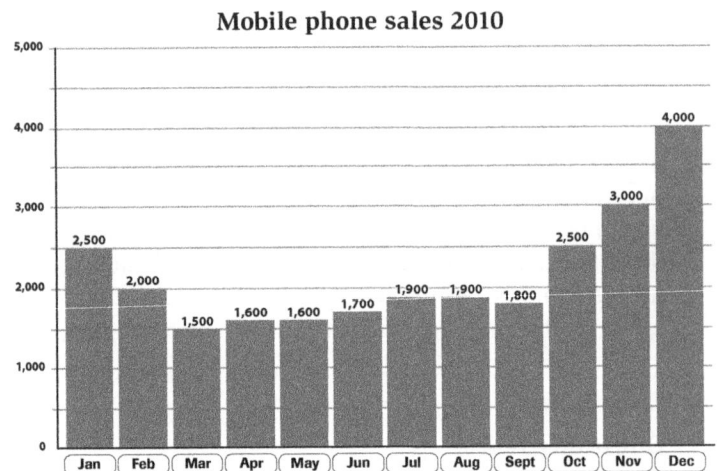

1 Sales of mobile phones showed a small rise ......in...... April.

2 The lowest sales were in the period .... March .... June.

3 .... March, sales of mobile phones fell .... 1,500.

4 This meant that sales fell .... 25% compared with the previous month.

5 .... a six-month period, there was a rise .... the number of new products launched.

6 .... October and December, there was an increase .... 60% .... sales of phones.

7 Sales of mobile phones rose .... 2,500 .... 4,000 .... that period.

8 Monthly sales peaked .... 4,000 .... December.

Writing Task 1

❶ Which of these descriptions best matches the graphs below? Circle A, B or C.

A The graphs below give information on the number of words spoken to children in various categories of family and the size of the vocabulary of those children.

B The graphs below compare the number of words children in different categories of family can understand with the number of words they use.

C The graphs below show rises in the vocabulary levels of both young children and older people in different categories of family.

Total words spoken to child

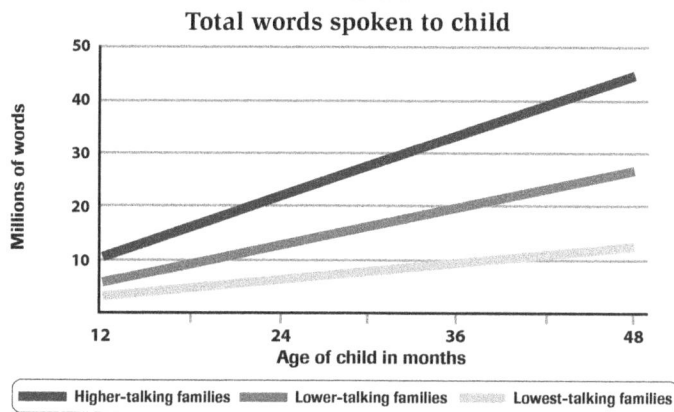

Children's total vocabulary size

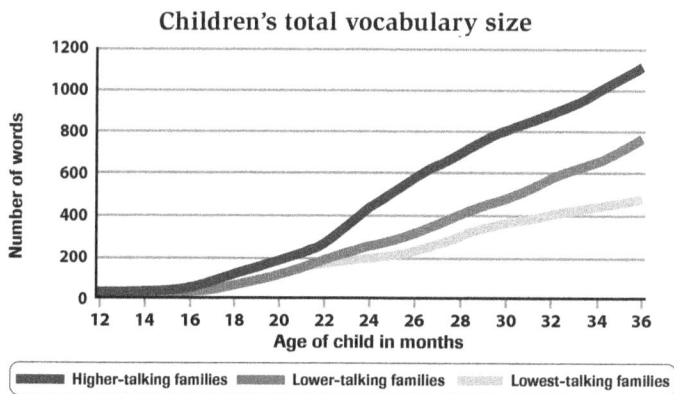

❷ Complete these sentences about the graphs with the correct information.

1 The number of words spoken to children in .... families rises from about 10 million to over 30 million between the ages of 12 months and 36 months.

2 The highest number of words spoken to any children aged 48 months is approximately ....

3 Children aged .... in the lowest-talking families hear approximately 10 million words.

4 The lowest vocabulary for any children aged 36 months is nearly .... words and the highest is approximately .... words.

5 The vocabulary of children in higher–talking families rises very steeply from the age of ....

6 Children in the .... families reach a vocabulary of 200 words at approximately the age of 26 months.

❸ Which of the following is the best overview of the information in the two graphs? Circle A, B or C.

A Young children in families that talk a lot increase their vocabulary much more quickly than young children in families that don't talk so much.

B The vocabulary of young children increases rapidly even if their families do not talk to them very much.

C The increase in a young child's vocabulary is not always linked to the amount of talking their families do.

❹ Look at this Writing task and write your answer.

The table below gives the results of two surveys, in 1997 and 2006, in which people were asked which communication skills were essential in their jobs.

Summarise the information by selecting and reporting the main features, and make comparisons where relevant.

Which communication skills are essential in your job? (Survey 1997 & 2006)

	Percentage of people asked	
Communication: External	1997	2006
Knowledge of particular products or services	35	41
Selling a product or service	24	21
Advising or caring for customers or clients	36	39
Dealing with people	60	65
Communication: Internal (within company)		
Instructing or training people	25	30
Persuading or influencing others	16	21
Making speeches or presentations	7	11
Analysing problems together with others	20	26
Planning the activities of others	14	15
Listening carefully to colleagues	38	47

Unit 4　New media

Reading　Section 1

❶ **Read through the article briefly. Then read Questions 1–6 and answer the following question.**

In which paragraphs will you find the information that you need to do this task? ....

❷ **Now read the text carefully and answer Questions 1–13.**

IS CONSTANT USE OF ELECTRONIC MEDIA CHANGING OUR MINDS?

The power of modern electronic media – the net, mobile phones and video games – to capture the attention of the human mind, particularly the young mind, and then distract it, has lately become a subject of concern. We are, say the worriers, losing the ability to apply ourselves properly to a single task, like reading a book in its entirety or mastering a piece of music on an instrument, with the result that our thinking is becoming shallower.

Nicholas Carr, the American science writer, has explored this theme for his new book, *The Shallows*, in which he argues that new media are not just changing our habits but our brain too. It turns out that the mature human brain is not an immutable seat of personality and intellect but a changeable thing, subject to 'neuroplasticity'. When our activities alter, so does the architecture of our brain. 'I'm

not thinking the way I used to think,' writes Carr. 'I feel it most strongly when I'm reading.' Years of internet use have, he suspects, dented his ability to read deeply, to absorb himself in books: 'My brain wasn't just drifting. It was hungry. It was demanding to be fed the way the net fed it.' He describes getting fidgety when faced with a long text: 'When we go online, we enter an environment that promotes cursory reading, hurried and distracted thinking, and superficial learning.'

Carr cites research by Gary Small, a professor of psychiatry at UCLA, who concluded that constant exposure to modern media strengthens new neural pathways while weakening older ones. Just five hours of internet use is enough to awaken previously dormant parts of the brain's pre-fontal cortex, concluded Small. For Carr, this is proof that the net can rewire the mind. He sees dangers. Deep thought, the ability to immerse oneself in an area of study, to follow a narrative, to understand an argument and develop a critique, is giving way to skimming. Young users of the Internet are good at drawing together information for a school project, for example, but that does not mean they have digested it.

But is a changing mind a more stupid one? Jake Vigdor and Helen Ladd are researchers at Duke University, North Carolina. In a study spanning five years and involving more than 100,000 children, they discovered a correlation between declining test scores in both mathematics and reading and the spread of home computers and broadband. 'The decline in scores was in the order of one or two percent but it was statistically significant,' says Vigdor. 'The drop may not be that great but one can say that the increase in computer use was certainly not positive.' The cut-off year for the study was 2005, when socialising was more primitive. Since then, social networking sites have become enormously powerful consumers of young people's time. Vigdor and Ladd concluded that the educational value of home computing was best realised when youngsters were actively supervised by parents.

This tendency to skim is compounded by the temptation of new media users to 'multi-task'. Watch a youngster on a computer and he could be Facebook-ing while burning a CD or Tweeting on his mobile phone. Modern management tends to promote multi-tasking as an expression of increased efficiency. Science, on the other hand, does not. The human brain is, it seems, not at all good at multi-tasking – unless it involves a highly developed skill like driving. David Meyer, a neuroscientist at the University of Michigan, says: 'The bottom line is that you can't simultaneously be thinking about your tax return and reading an essay, just as you can't talk to yourself about two things at once. People may think otherwise but it's a myth. With complicated tasks, you will never, ever be able to overcome the inherent limitations in the brain.'

Paying attention is the prerequisite of memory: the sharper the attention, the sharper the memory. Cursory study born of the knowledge that information is easily available online results, say the worriers, in a failure to digest it. In addition, the brain needs rest and recovery time to consolidate thoughts. Teenagers who fill every moment with a text or Tweet are not allowing their minds necessary downtime. All rather worrying, but is it that bad?

We have been here before, of course. The Ancient Greeks lamented the replacement of the oral tradition with written text, and the explosion in book ownership resulting from the printing press was, for some, a disaster. In the 18th century, a French statesman railed against a new device that turned people into 'dispersed' individuals, isolated in 'sullen silence'. He was talking about the newspaper.

The net is supposed to consume the lives of young people, yet the only reliable studies about the time spent online, collated by the World Health Organization, suggest children spend between two and four hours in front of screens, including television screens, and not six or seven, as often suggested. Moreover, there is evidence that youngsters who use social networking sites have more rewarding offline social lives than those who do not.

A study on children and new technology in the UK included a 'study of studies' by Professor David Buckingham of the University of London's Institute of Education. He concluded: 'Broadly speaking, the evidence about the effects of new media is weak and inconclusive – and this applies to both positive and negative effects.'

Certainly the 'old' media don't seem to be doing that badly. An annual survey shows that sales of children's books this year were 4.9 per cent greater than last year, with more than 60 million sold. The damage, if any, done by excessive computer time may not be so much to do with what is being done online as what is being missed – time spent with family or playing in trees with friends.

Questions 1–6

Do the following statements agree with the information given in the reading passage?

Write

TRUE   *if the statement agrees with the information*

FALSE   *if the statement contradicts the information*

NOT GIVEN   *if there is no information on this*

1   Some people believe that modern electronic media only have a negative effect on young people.

2   Nicholas Carr's book on the subject is a bestseller.

3   Nicholas Carr believes that electronic media have affected his enjoyment of reading books.

4   Gary Small's research supports Nicholas Carr's beliefs.

5   Management beliefs on multi-tasking are proved correct by scientific research.

6   David Meyer's views on the limitations of the brain have caused controversy.

Questions 7–10

Complete the notes below.

Choose **NO MORE THAN TWO WORDS AND/OR A NUMBER** *from the passage for each answer.*

Vigdor and Ladd's research

* looked at over **7** ....

* found that lower **8** .... and home computer use were linked

* indicated that the effects of greater home computer use could not be described as **9** ....

* concluded that **10** .... should be involved in home computer use

Answer the questions below.

Choose NO MORE THAN TWO WORDS AND/OR A NUMBER from the passage for each answer.

11 Which invention was criticised by an 18th century French politician?

12 According to studies that can be trusted, what is the maximum amount of time per day that children spend looking at screens?

13 Which products have become more popular recently?

Listening Part 4

❶ **You will hear an expert giving a talk on blogs. Look at Questions 6–10 and answer the following question.**

Which three questions need a noun

to fill the gap? ....

❷ ⓞ⑤ **Now listen and answer Questions 1–10.**

Questions 1–5

Complete the summary below.

Write ONE OR TWO WORDS for each answer.

Blogs and the History of Blogging

A blog can perhaps be best described as a website that consists of a kind of journal that is regularly updated. Blogs cover a very wide variety of topics and many of them are personal diaries. Blogs are usually not **1** .... because they have interactive elements, which may lead to friendships or even **2** .... relationships between people.

The first 'blog' was probably created in 1994 by a student and he called it his '**3** .... '. Similar websites were then created and these included both links and **4** .... In 1999, someone changed the term used for these websites by creating the phrase '**5** ....', and therefore invented the term 'blog'.

Questions 6–10

Complete the flow chart below.

Write ONE WORD ONLY for each answer.

Blogging Workflow – Advice

Decide what the **6** .... of your posts will be

⬇

Do some reading before starting a post

⬇

As you compose the post, keep a record of **7** .... and links

⬇

After creating the post, add some tags to it to improve searchability

⬇

Use social networking sites to **8** .... a post you think is outstanding

⬇

Look at the **9** .... relating to the post

⬇

Don't simply say **10** .... to people who have responded to your post

⬇

Go on to other blogs and leave comments.

Vocabulary

Cause, factor and *reason*

❶ Complete the sentences with *causes, reasons* or *factors*.

1 Illegal internet downloading is one of the main .... of the problems faced by record companies.

2 One of the .... why fewer people buy newspapers these days is that they can read them online.

3 When considering which computer to get, reliability is one of the key ....

4 Children like computer games for a number of .... , for example, because the graphics are exciting.

5 The results of this problem are known but what are the .... ?

6 Price and number of applications are among the .... that determine how popular a digital product becomes.

▶ Student's Book unit 4, p42

❷ Complete the sentences about internet use with the jumbled words in the box.

WBOESR	CUHOT	NODDAWLO	~~TCAH~~
ETAD	SIVTI	HRCAERSE	ITGKNREOWN

- I often **(1)** ....*chat*........ to friends on a social **(2)** .... site. I like to keep up to **(3)** .... with what everyone's doing and I check the site for messages several times a day.

- I need to **(4)** .... this topic and I'm going to **(5)** .... various documents from a number of places.

- I often **(6)** .... the Internet for long periods of time and **(7)** .... lots of different sites.

- I use internet news sites to keep in **(8)** .... with world events.

Key vocabulary

❸ Complete the sentences below with the verbs in the box. Two of the verbs do not fit into any of the gaps.

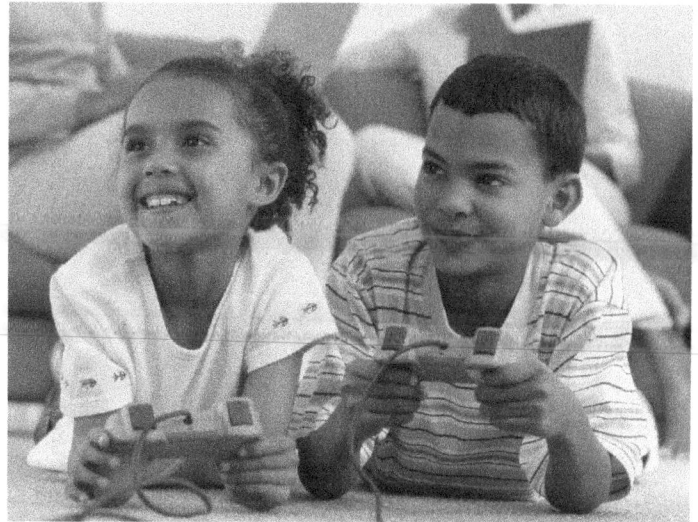

do	experiment	reveal	launch	evolve	transform
carry	attract	turn	lack	restrict	~~discourage~~

1 Parents try to ...*discourage*... their children from using computers too much.

2 Did people realise that computers would completely .... the way we live?

3 Some children who spend a lot of time on computers may .... the incentive to go out and make friends face to face.

4 Stories about the dangers of internet use .... attention when they appear in the media.

5 Experts .... a lot of research on how people use computers.

6 Statistics .... that some children spend many hours a day in front of screens.

7 Some parents try to .... the amount of time their children use the Internet.

8 Whenever companies .... new games consoles, children want to buy them.

9 Children like to .... with new gadgets to find out what they can do.

10 How will the way people use computers .... over the next few decades?

Writing Task 2

1 **Read this Writing task and underline the main points.**

> Write about the following topic:
>
> *The use of electronic media has a negative effect on personal relationships between people.*
>
> *To what extent do you agree or disagree?*
>
> Give reasons for your answer and include any relevant examples from your knowledge or experience.

2 **What *must* your answer include? Write *Yes* or *No* in the spaces next to each choice.**

A a mention of at least one kind of electronic media ....

B your opinion on whether the statement is true or not ....

C your favourite kinds of electronic media ....

D how the use of electronic media can affect personal relationships ....

E which forms of electronic media are the most expensive ....

F a comparison between young people and older people ....

G how people interact using electronic media ....

H a prediction about future use of electronic media ....

3 **Which of these notes for the above task are relevant and could be included in an answer and which are not? Write *Yes* or *No*.**

A people don't speak to each other face to face ....

B people sometimes don't read or reply to emails and texts ....

C some electronic gadgets quickly become old-fashioned ....

D some people make lots of friends on social networking sites ....

E some electronic gadgets are more popular than others ....

F people sometimes send messages without thinking first ....

G people can keep in touch regularly using electronic media ....

H some people don't know how to use electronic media ....

4 **Now write your answer for the Writing task above.**

Grammar

However, although, even and *on the other hand*

▶ Student's Book unit 4, p44

❶ Decide which of the following sentences about using the Internet for research is correct. Sometimes more than one choice may be correct.

1 A The Internet is often a good place for research, however other sources of information can be better.
   B Although the Internet is often a good place for research, other sources of information can be better.
   C The Internet is often a good place for research. Even though, other sources of information can be better.

2 A There's a lot of information on the Internet. On the other hand, some of it isn't accurate.
   B There's a lot of information on the Internet. Although, some of it isn't accurate.
   C There's a lot of information on the Internet. However, some of it isn't accurate.

3 A You can find a lot of useful information on the web, although it can take a long time to find it.
   B You can find a lot of useful information on the web, even though it can take a long time to find it.
   C You can find a lot of useful information on the web however it can take a long time to find it.

4 A However internet research is useful, it's not always the best kind of research.
   B Internet research is useful on the other hand it's not always the best kind of research.
   C Even though internet research is useful, it's not always the best kind of research.

Articles

❷ Choose the correct options.

1 I really want to go to *a /an* university in the U.S.
2 *A / The* music industry in Britain wants *the / a* government to stop illegal downloading.
3 I spend *a / an* hour on Facebook every morning before I go to college.
4 My sister starts *a / –* university in September.
5 Can you imagine *the / –* life without *an / the* Internet?
6 I found *a / the* brilliant website last night. I've emailed all my friends about *the / a* site.
7 Do you have *the / –* arguments with your family about who can use your home computer?
8 *The / A* first thing to do when you want to start a blog is to decide on the topic.
9 *– / The* quickest way to contact *the / –* friends is by texting them.
10 *– / The* young are always keen to try new technology.

❸ Complete the following paragraph with *a, an, the* or *–* (if there is no article).

It is extraordinary how quickly (1) .....*the*..... Internet and email have become (2) .... enormous part of everyone's lives. Not so many years ago, people didn't have (3) .... PCs and (4) .... computers were very big objects that only existed in (5) .... big companies and organisations. When it was (6) .... new invention, only (7) .... rich could afford (8) .... PC. But now almost everyone has (9) .... home computer and they have changed (10) .... people's lives. Instead of making (11) .... phone call or writing (12) .... letter, they send (13) .... email. They use them at (14) .... work and (15) .... children use them at (16) .... school. In a very short time, they have become (17) .... most important tool in (18) .... world.

The world in our hands

Listening Part 1

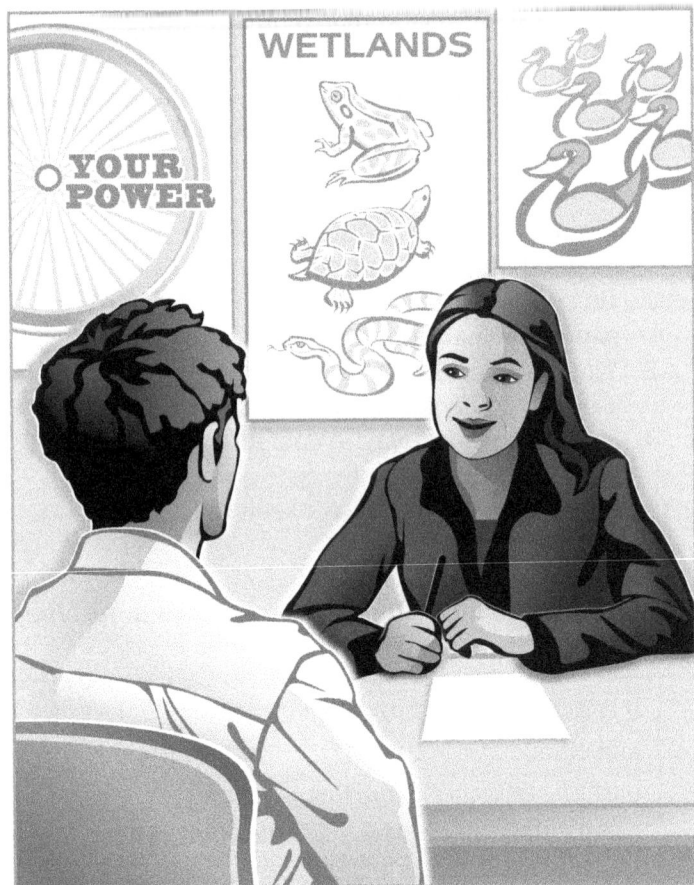

❶ **Look at the first task, Questions 1–6.**

Which questions might need a number **only** for the answer? ....

❷ (06) **Now listen and answer Questions 1–10.**

Questions 1–6

Complete the notes below.

Write **NO MORE THAN TWO WORDS AND/OR A NUMBER** *for each answer.*

The Volunteer Agency

- has recruited **1** .... people for environmental projects
- project abroad involves doing
  2 .... or going into the rain forest
- major project for dealing with
  3 .... in the countryside
- project for improving conditions for
  4 ....
- **5** .... projects in urban areas
- some projects do not have any
  6 ....

Questions 7–10

Complete the table below.

Write **ONE WORD** *for each answer.*

Name of organisation	Numbers	Example volunteer activity
Wildlife Link	24,000 volunteers	getting information about **7** .... of wildlife
Wildlife Watch	300 **8**	doing administrative work
9 .... Earth	908 projects	building **10** .... and walls

Vocabulary

Nature, the environment or *the countryside?*
Tourist or *tourism?*

❶ Complete the sentences by putting *nature,
environment, countryside, tourist* or *tourism* in
each gap.

1 .... is the biggest industry in some
countries.

2 If you are a 'responsible ....', you try
to make sure that you don't do damage to the
.... in the country you are visiting.

3 People who like .... enjoy getting out of
cities and going to the ....

4 From our room we had a wonderful view over
spectacular ....

5 Increases in .... can sometimes have a
bad effect on places.

Key vocabulary

❷ Complete the sentences, using the nouns in the
box.

plant   step   drawback   ~~challenge~~
infrastructure   source

1 Solving that environmental problem is a big
...*challenge*... and will take a long time.

2 You have to create a proper .... for the
supply of alternative energy supplies.

3 What kind of power .... should be built
to supply energy?

4 Can solar energy ever be a major .... of
electricity?

5 The high cost is a major .... of that
kind of power.

6 After reducing emissions, the next ....
is to use alternative energy supplies.

❸ Complete the sentences below connected with
environmental issues, using words from the
wordsearch.

C	L	C	H	A	N	G	E	S	S	I	E
D	E	S	A	T	O	V	A	T	I	N	M
E	L	S	B	M	T	U	R	O	N	B	I
S	A	Y	I	O	I	P	E	P	F	E	S
T	O	U	T	S	W	I	N	C	O	T	S
R	L	H	A	P	H	L	E	A	S	I	I
U	N	C	T	H	I	E	W	A	S	P	O
C	O	N	S	E	R	V	A	T	I	O	N
T	U	Y	R	R	O	E	B	A	L	K	S
I	N	T	E	E	V	L	L	S	S	I	P
O	L	R	I	N	G	S	E	M	I	D	S
N	E	N	D	A	N	G	E	R	E	D	O

1 What can be done to protect the
......*endangered*...... species of the world before
they die out?

2 Is it possible to cut down on the use of
.... fuels?

3 Which .... energy sources can
replace the energy sources currently used?

4 Is it possible to stop the .... of
rainforests?

5 Has the problem of climate ....
been caused by human activity?

6 A lot of damage is done when greenhouse gases
are released into the ....

7 It is becoming harder for some species to survive
in their natural ....

8 Scientists and designers are trying to design cars
with zero ....

9 There are wildlife ....
programmes to protect various species.

10 There is some evidence that rising sea
.... are happening in various
parts of the world.

Reading Section 2

❶ **Read through the text about Russia's boreal forests briefly and look at Questions 6–9.**

In which sections of the text are the scientists on the list mentioned? ....

❷ **Now read the text carefully and answer Questions 1–13.**

Russia's boreal forests and wild grasses could combat climate change

A Scientists believe Russia's ancient forests are the country's best natural weapon against climate change, even though the stockpile of carbon beneath the ground also makes these areas vulnerable to carbon release. A recent study found that half the world's carbon is stored within land in the permafrost region, about two-thirds of which lies in Russia. Overlying former glaciers, they are a coniferous mix called the boreal forest. 'There's a lot of carbon there and it's very vulnerable,' says Josep Canadell, co-author of the study. 'If the permafrost thaws, we could be releasing ten percent more carbon a year for several centuries more than our previous models predicted. It's going to cost a lot to reduce our emissions by that much – but it will cost more in damage if we don't.'

B The study was published in *Global Biogeochemical Cycles*. Researchers found that the region contains 1,672 billion tons of organic carbon, much of it several feet underground, that 'would account for approximately 50 percent of the estimated global below-ground organic carbon'. Another paper published in *Nature* found that old forests, which make up perhaps half of the boreal forest, 'continue to accumulate carbon, contrary to the long-standing view that they are carbon-neutral'. Even though fires and insect infestations destroy entire swaths of forest and release into the atmosphere the carbon they contain, old-growth forests still take in more than these natural disturbances release, says lead author Sebastiaan Luyssaert, a biologist at the University of Antwerp in Belgium. 'This is all the more reason to protect Russia's boreal forests,' which take in 500 million tons of carbon a year, or about one-fifth of the carbon absorbed by the world's landmass, says Mr Canadell, who is executive director of the Global Carbon Project, based in Canberra.

C Jing Ming Chen, a University of Toronto geography professor who specialises in climate modelling for the boreal region, says: 'Cutting boreal trees increases the amount of carbon in the atmosphere and it takes 50 to 100 years to put that carbon back in the ground.' Luysaaert and Chen argue there's a strong case for conserving the old-growth forests. 'It's better to keep as much carbon in the forest as possible right now,' Mr Luyssaert explains. 'If we want to avoid irreversible processes like melting permafrost or changing ocean currents, we absolutely have to control our emissions in the next two or three decades. It's a case where you need to be short-sighted to be far-sighted.' 'The threats to the boreal forests don't seem significant right now,' explains Nigel Roulet, a carbon cycle specialist at McGill University in Montreal, 'but I'm convinced pressure will increase as the region gets warmer and it gets easier to operate there. Also, I expect these resources to become more valuable as others are exhausted.'

D Scientists say Russia and Kazakhstan could make a unique contribution to the fight against global warming by harvesting wild grasses that have overgrown 100,000 square miles of agricultural lands abandoned in the nineties, and using them to make ethanol – or, better yet, burn them in coal-fuelled power plants. According to Nicolas Vuichard, principal author of a paper published in *Environmental Science and Technology* of Washington, DC, using the grasses to make ethanol would sequester in the ground, over 60 years, about 10 million tons of carbon a year – one-quarter as dead root matter in the soil and the rest in producing ethanol as a substitute for petroleum-based fuels. 'That's not huge on a world scale, but it's substantial,' he says. Fossil fuels emit about eight billion tons of carbon a year, of which about two billion tons are absorbed by plants and soil.

E Renton Righelato, visiting research fellow at the University of Reading and former chairman of the World Land Trust, agrees. 'Given that it would take the world's entire supply of arable land to replace just two-thirds of our transport fuel needs,' he says, 'biofuels are not a practicable long-term solution for transportation emissions. What we need is carbon-free fuel. But in the case of abandoned croplands, using grasses as biofuels could make a contribution,' he adds. Study co-author Adam Wolf, of the Carnegie Institution for Science at Stanford University, cites a study by Elliott Campbell in *Science* magazine that showed that burning grasses in a coal-fuelled plant doubles the savings in carbon emissions compared to using the same grasses to make ethanol. 'If biofuels are going to reduce emissions, using abandoned croplands to make electricity and offset coal use is our best bet,' he says. 'Both of these countries have coal-fuelled power plants, so the process could start soon.' Thus, Russia and Kazakhstan are now in a position to become leaders in green energy, and could use the grasses to export clean electricity in addition to oil and gas, according to Mr Wolf.

Questions 1–5

The reading passage has five paragraphs, **A–E**.

Which paragraph contains the following information?

*Write the correct letter, **A–E**.*

NB *You may use any letter more than once.*

1. a view concerning what can and what cannot replace something
2. a mention of the amount by which carbon emissions might increase in the future
3. a reference to an established belief that researchers say is incorrect
4. evidence from one study that supports the conclusions of another study
5. how much carbon is currently located in a particular part of the world

Questions 6–9

Look at the following statements (Questions 6–9) and the list of scientists below.

*Match each statement with the correct scientist, **A–D**.*

6. More attention will be paid to the situation in the boreal forests in the future.
7. Boreal forests are able to deal with some of the damage that is done to them.
8. Earlier research may have underestimated the scale of a future problem.
9. The damage done by destroying boreal forests lasts for a very long time.

List of scientists

A Josep Canadell	**C** Jing Ming Chen
B Sebastiaan Luyssaert	**D** Nigel Roulet

Questions 10–13

Complete the summary below.

*Choose **NO MORE THAN TWO WORDS** from the passage for each answer.*

Wild grasses in Russia and Kazakhstan

Scientists believe that wild grasses which are currently growing on former **10** .... in Russia and Kazakhstan could be useful in combating environmental problems. There are two different ideas concerning how this could happen.

With the first idea, approximately ten million tons of carbon would be stored in the ground, and three-quarters of this would create **11** .... that could be used instead of petroleum-based fuels. The second idea is to burn the grasses in **12** .... power plants. Supporters of this idea say that the effect in reducing carbon emissions would be twice as great as if the first idea was carried out. The grasses would be used to produce **13** .... and production of this could begin in a short period of time.

Writing Task 1

❶ Look at the Writing task below. Which of the following *must* you mention in your answer? Write *Yes* or *No*.

A different types of buildings ....

B different types of energy produced ....

C distances ....

D differences between two systems ....

E who uses the energy produced ....

F opinions on each system ....

G the results of each system ....

H stages in each system ....

The diagram below compares two different systems of energy production – a conventional system and one that uses natural gas as the source of power.

Summarise the information by reporting the main features, and make comparisons where relevant.

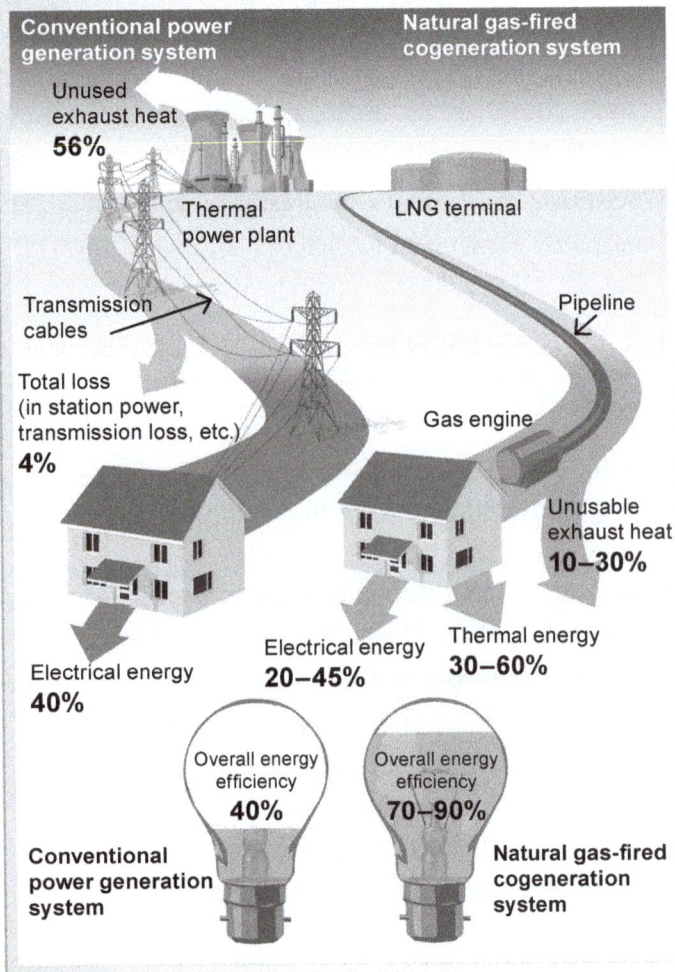

Conventional power generation system

Natural gas-fired cogeneration system

Unused exhaust heat **56%**

Thermal power plant

LNG terminal

Transmission cables

Pipeline

Total loss (in station power, transmission loss, etc.) **4%**

Gas engine

Unusable exhaust heat **10–30%**

Electrical energy **40%**

Electrical energy **20–45%**

Thermal energy **30–60%**

Overall energy efficiency **40%**

Overall energy efficiency **70–90%**

Conventional power generation system

Natural gas-fired cogeneration system

---

❷ Complete this sample answer for the Writing task with words or figures.

The diagram compares two different ways of producing energy. The conventional system involves a thermal power plant. At the first stage, at the plant, **(1)** .... of the energy put into the system is not used and becomes waste heat. At the next stage, power goes from the plant through **(2)** .... and at this stage another **(3)** .... of the energy is lost. This means that only **(4)** .... of the power is used at the end of the process and this is used as **(5)** .... In the other system, natural gas is used as the source of power. Power comes from the **(6)** .... through a **(7)** .... to a gas engine. At this stage, between 10% and 30% of the energy that has been produced is lost. Of the power that is not lost, **(8)** .... of it is then used for **(9)** .... energy and 20-45% is used as electrical energy. The comparison shows that the conventional system is less energy efficient than the other system, called a **(10)** .... system. The overall energy efficiency of the conventional system is only 40%, meaning that only **(11)** .... of the power it produces can be used. In contrast, the system based on natural gas is much more efficient, as between **(12)** .... of the energy produced is used.

❸ Now divide the sample answer into four paragraphs. One of the paragraphs is very short. Put // to indicate where a new paragraph starts. Divide it in this way:

Paragraph 1: Introduction

Paragraph 2: Description of system

Paragraph 3: Description of system

Paragraph 4: Overview

4 Look at the Writing task below. What does the diagram show? Circle A, B or C.

A stages in a process

B how something happens

C how to do something

> The diagram below shows how heat is lost and energy wasted in a house because of air getting into and out of the house.
> Summarise the information by reporting the main features and make comparisons where appropriate.

Air leaks and heat loss in houses

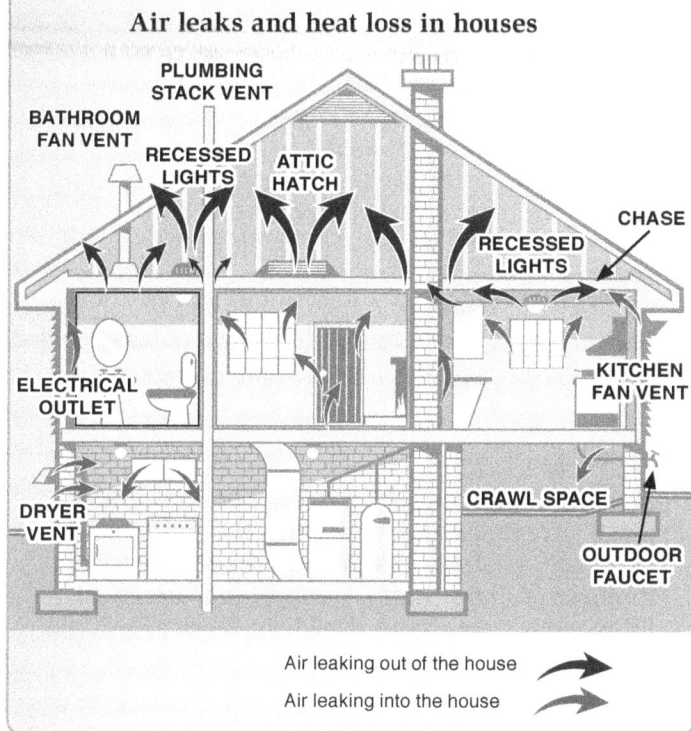

PLUMBING STACK VENT
BATHROOM FAN VENT
RECESSED LIGHTS
ATTIC HATCH
CHASE
RECESSED LIGHTS
KITCHEN FAN VENT
ELECTRICAL OUTLET
DRYER VENT
CRAWL SPACE
OUTDOOR FAUCET

Air leaking out of the house
Air leaking into the house

5 Now write your answer for the Writing task above.

Grammar

The passive

1 Complete these sentences about a local recycling scheme with the correct passive phrases in the box.

should be placed	is taken	will be informed
are provided	~~was introduced~~	can be collected
have been increased	must be sorted	

1 The scheme ....was introduced.... two years ago.

2 Collections .... to twice a week.

3 Containers for household waste
.... by the council.

4 All waste .... into categories.

5 Paper .... in the blue boxes.

6 Larger items for recycling .... if you phone this number.

7 The waste .... to a recycling plant.

8 Households .... of any changes to collection days.

2 Complete the second sentence so that it has a similar meaning to the first sentence, using the correct form of the passive.

1 a Nowadays they teach children about environmental issues at school.

 b Nowadays ....children are taught........... about environmental issues at school.

2 a The authorities have started recycling schemes throughout the country.

 b .... throughout the country.

3 a Governments have discussed international cooperation on environmental issues.

 b .... by governments.

4 a Experts say that people should do more to solve environmental problems.

 b Experts say that .... to solve environmental problems.

5 a One idea is that people can use solar power to provide energy.

 b One idea is that .... to provide energy.

6 a We must find alternatives to existing energy sources soon.

 b .... soon.

7 a Some countries took steps to deal with environmental problems years ago.

 b .... by some countries to deal with environmental problems years ago.

8 a Will we solve environmental problems in the future?

 b .... in the future?

Making money, spending money

Reading Section 1

❶ Read through the article briefly and answer the following question.

What is it about? Circle A, B or C.

A   two people who own shops

B   various different products

C   a chain of shops and a product

❷ Now read the text carefully and answer Questions 1–13.

MOVERS AND SHAKERS

Discover the stories behind two enthusiastic entrepreneurs who are creating major waves in the UK business world

Retailers often declare that customers are their most important asset. But, while some sound as if they are paying lip service to the idea, **Sally Bailey**, chief executive of **White Stuff**, is a true believer. Even the clothing retailer's website reflects her view, declaring: 'Lovely clothes for lovely people'. Ms Bailey says: 'The most important people are those who buy our product. This includes the buyers who select it, and the customers who buy it in our shops. Everything we do is about service to get the product into the customer's hands.'

So when research revealed that customers disliked changing rooms that opened directly onto the shop floor, White Stuff amended its floor plans, introducing a false wall that screened off the changing area. 'It's not rocket science,' explains Ms Bailey. 'You just need to listen to what the customer is saying. We are dedicated to pleasing them. We ask: "What is the best thing we could do?"' Hence, the introduction of one oversized fitting room in each of White Stuff's 54 stores to enable mothers to bring their buggies in while they change.

'When a customer walks into a White Stuff shop, we want them to feel like they are at home,' says Ms Bailey. 'There are chairs to sit down on, water coolers, and staff will come along with colouring books to entertain children while the customer browses.' Even the background music is carefully considered. On Saturdays it has a faster tempo. On Sundays, when customers may prefer a quieter atmosphere, the tone is softer. 'The music is changed by the hour, according to the day,' says Ms Bailey.

White Stuff has eschewed the shop design of a traditional fashion retailer, preferring to model its interiors on a Victorian house where Ms Bailey believes her customers aspire to live. Since her arrival, White Stuff has sought locations away from the beaten track and shopping centres are viewed as anathema. 'To be honest, we do have some stores that are very hard to find,' says Ms Bailey. 'In Exeter, for example, there's the High Street and the shopping centre, but you have to turn left down an alley to find White Stuff, right by an organic butcher and coffee shop.'

Yet White Stuff's customers, whom Ms Bailey describes as 'extremely loyal', are not deterred by these intrepid expeditions. When she took over five years ago, White Stuff had 15 stores and an annual turnover of £14m. Today, turnover is in excess of £55m, with stores generating annual revenues between £500,000 and £2.5m from an average customer spend of £35.

Matt Stockdale, managing director of **HomePride**, which this year will turn over more than £4m, has the mother of former Tesco buyer Fraser McDonald to thank for his success. Desperate to get the supermarket chain to stock his oven cleaning product, Oven Pride, Mr Stockdale bombarded the buyer with calls.

But it was to no avail: 'The response was always "Thanks but no thanks",' he recalls. 'So I said, "Let me send some to your mother, your aunt, your grandmother…" and, I think to make me go away, he gave me his mother's address.' Two weeks later, Mr Stockdale was in the buyer's office signing a deal to supply his product to 30 stores. 'He told me that his mother wanted him to give me a chance but that he didn't give me much hope,' says Mr Stockdale. A year later he was supplying 130 Tesco stores. 'I didn't realise when I first approached Tesco that it was the

UK's biggest supermarket chain,' says Mr Stockdale. 'I just knew that I shopped there.'

The idea for the oven cleaner came in 1999 when, after being made redundant from his job as a sales manager for a telecoms business, Mr Stockdale decided to fulfil a lifelong ambition to run his own company. 'I looked at a catalogue business first because direct sales was what I knew,' he says. 'But I came across chemical companies making products, one of which was an oven cleaner. I was always the one lumbered with cleaning our oven, so I was intrigued.' He tested one product, a bottle of white fluid, which produced such great results that he started to research the oven cleaner marketplace. 'I found the hardest thing was to clean the racks,' says Mr Stockdale.

He decided to create kits to make cleaning racks easy, sourcing packaging, disposable gloves and a bag, into which the racks could be placed with the cleaning fluid. 'I created 5,000 units and sent one each to Kleeneze, Betterware and QVC, and got nowhere,' he recalls. Dejected, Mr Stockdale found another sales job but, 15 months later, a fax arrived with a purchase order from Kleeneze. 'I went to the garage and dusted down the stock,' he says. Kleeneze sold out within weeks, and placed more orders. Then QVC faxed across an order. 'I was suddenly on national television, but in eight weeks QVC had sold out,' he says. 'I didn't realise what I had.' It took a letter from a satisfied customer, asking when the cleaner would be available in shops, to prompt Mr Stockdale to change his strategy and approach high street retailers. Enter Tesco.

In its first year, HomePride turned over £90,000 but soon reached £1.1m. 'Going into retail changed everything for me,' says Mr Stockdale.

Questions 1–3

Label the diagram below.

Choose **NO MORE THAN TWO WORDS** *from the passage for each answer.*

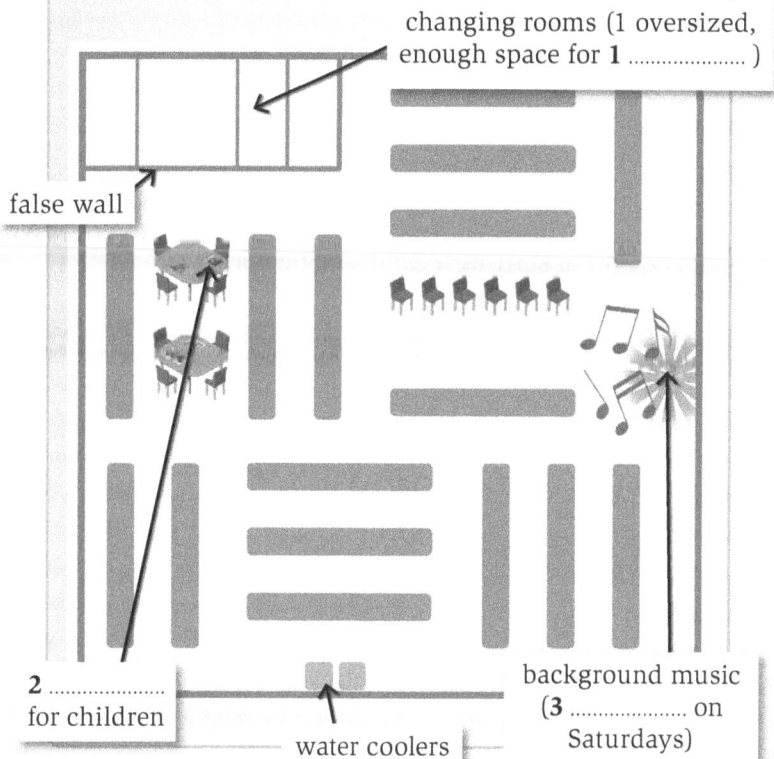

changing rooms (1 oversized, enough space for **1** ....)

false wall

2 ....
for children

water coolers

background music (**3** .... on Saturdays)

Questions 4–8

Do the following statements agree with the information given in the reading passage?

Write

TRUE	*if the statement agrees with the information*
FALSE	*if the statement contradicts the information*
NOT GIVEN	*if there is no information on this*

4 Sally Bailey intends to find locations for White Stuff in shopping centres.

5 Sally Bailey started White Stuff.

6 The buyer at Tesco initially rejected Oven Pride.

7 The buyer's mother often gives him advice on products.

8 Matt Stockdale discovered important information about Tesco after contacting the company.

Complete the flow chart below.

Choose **NO MORE THAN TWO WORDS AND/OR A NUMBER** *from the passage for each answer.*

The story of HomePride

Matt Stockdale made redundant from job in telecoms

↓

Thought of starting a catalogue business (experience in **9** ....)

↓

Saw chemical products and became interested in oven cleaners

↓

Tested a white fluid for cleaning ovens and researched the market

↓

Observed that the biggest problem was how to get **10** .... clean

↓

Made **11** .... to solve this problem

↓

Sent his product to various companies

↓

First order came after **12** ....

↓

Product appeared on TV and sold out

↓

A question asked by a **13** .... gave him the idea of approaching shops

Vocabulary

Verbs + infinitive and verbs + -ing

❶ Complete these sentences about money, using the infinitive or –ing forms of the verbs in the box.

lose	check	buy	~~pay~~	put
spend	save	borrow		

1 I refuse ....*to pay*....... such a high price for a ticket.

2 I ended up .... all my money in that shop because there were so many things I liked.

3 I tried .... some money but nobody agreed to lend me any.

4 Did you remember .... some money into your account today?

5 I wanted .... money, so I bought a cheaper one.

6 If you don't want to risk .... your money, don't gamble.

7 She failed .... the price before she bought it and it cost more than she expected.

8 Those phones are not worth .... , they're not very good.

❷ Complete the second sentence so that it has a similar meaning to the first sentence.

1 a He often gets into trouble with money.
   b He keeps .....*getting*..... into trouble with money.

2 a I got a job, so I was able to earn some money.
   b Getting a job enabled .... some money.

3 a I was surprised that prices there were so high.
   b I didn't expect .... so high.

4 a I don't want to spend a lot of money.
   b I want to avoid .... a lot of money.

5 a 'Buy this model,' the shop assistant said to me.
   b The shop assistant advised .... that model.

6 a 'Pay the bill before the end of the week,' she said to me.
   b She reminded .... the bill before the end of the week.

7 a I think I might get a new computer.

   b I'm considering .... a new computer.

8 a My parents said that I should save money.

   b My parents encouraged .... money.

▶ Student's Book unit 6, p61

❸ Complete these sentences about banks and banking with the jumbled words in the box.

TRDEFOAVR   TCERID   SRIETENT
TFIRR̶̶   QLAFRNA   NRAHCR̶

1 I checked the ....*balance*.... to see how much money I had in my account.

2 My account was in .... , so I had some money to spend.

3 The .... rate on this account has fallen recently.

4 There's always a long queue in the local .... of my bank.

5 If you pay the bill by direct .... , it's a bit cheaper.

6 He's got a big .... at the bank and other money problems too.

Key vocabulary

❹ Choose the correct option, A, B or C, to complete each sentence.

1 If you buy a branded product, it
   A is cheaper than usual.
   B has the maker's name on it.
   C is being specially advertised.

2 If you purchase something, you
   A buy it.
   B look for it.
   C use it.

3 An own-label product is a product that
   A is new on the market.
   B is for sale at a cheaper price.
   C has the shop's name on it.

4 Retailer can be another word for
   A product.
   B shop.
   C customer.

Listening Part 2

❶ You are going to hear a manager talking about new machines in a museum. Look at Questions 5–10. Which of the following are you required to label? Circle A, B or C.

A the kinds of drink in the machine

B how you order a drink from the machine

C how you put drinks into the machine

❷ (07) Now listen and answer Questions 1–10.

Questions 1–4

Where will the following machines be?

Choose **FOUR** *answers from the box and write the correct letter,* **A–F**, *next to questions 1–4.*

1 cash machine ....   3 games machine ....

2 ticket machine ....   4 drinks machine ....

A visitor centre	D entrance hall
B in front of the building	E exhibition halls
C next to elevators	F reception area

Questions 5–10

Label the diagram below.

Write **ONE OR TWO WORDS AND/OR A NUMBER** *for each answer.*

DRINKS MACHINE FOR STAFF ROOM

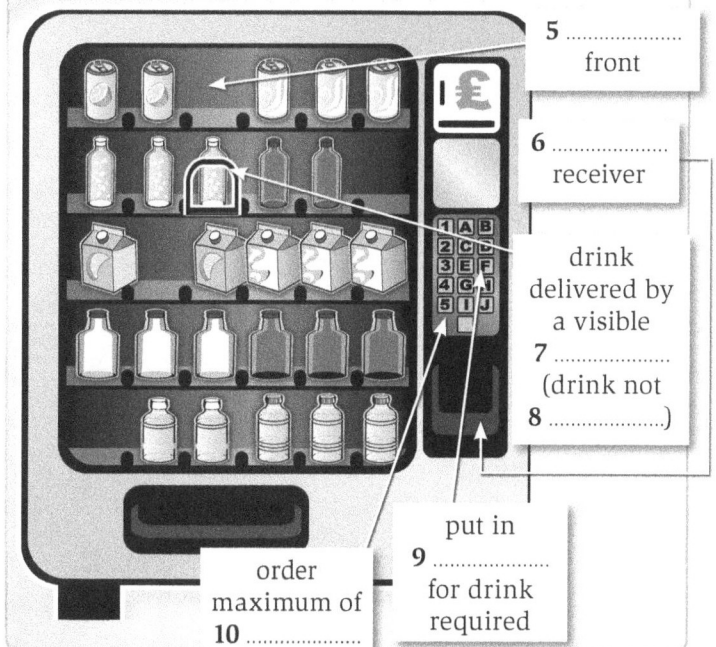

5 ....
front

6 ....
receiver

drink delivered by a visible

7 ....
(drink not

8 ....)

put in

order maximum of
10 ....

9 ....
for drink required

Writing Task 2

1 Read the following Writing task and underline the main points to consider.

Write about the following topic:

The purpose of businesses is to make money and they should concentrate only on this.

Do you agree or disagree?

Give reasons for your answer and include any relevant examples from your knowledge or experience.

2 Look at these student ideas for paragraphs. Which of these ideas would make suitable paragraphs for an answer? Write *Yes* or *No*.

A businesses and the environment ....

B the most successful business sectors ....

C how to start a business ....

D the need to make profits ....

E why some businesses fail ....

F treatment of employees ....

G why people choose a particular career ....

H businesses and the local community ....

3 The following are phrases that could be used in an answer to this Writing task. Complete them with the correct prepositions.

1 making money is an important part ..*of*.. what companies do

2 businesses play an important role .... society

3 businesses want to make profits .... what they produce

4 companies that lose a lot of money can go .... business

5 companies do business .... other companies

6 a company's attitude .... the people who work for it

7 businesses should also make a contribution .... society

8 companies should pay attention .... other matters

9 profitable companies may take .... more workers

10 businesses need to give thought .... other matters

4 Now write your answer for the Writing task above.

Grammar

Relative pronouns and relative clauses

1 Complete these sentences about shopping with relative pronouns.

1 The town ....*where*....... I live has lots of shops.

2 The shops .... I like most are all local.

3 The people .... work in the local shops are all friendly.

4 My favourite shop is the clothes shop .... I buy most of my clothes.

5 I first went there ten years ago, ... I was a teenager.

6 It sells clothes by designers .... clothes I really like.

7 It has assistants .... are very friendly and helpful.

8 And it sells clothes at prices .... I can afford!

❷ Complete this description of someone's job with the relative clauses in the box.

> where there is a problem   when he left
> which is   which need   ~~whose name is~~
> who don't know   which describe   which involves

The mystery shopper

I have a friend (1) ....*whose name is*.... Graham. He has

a job (2) .... very interesting. He started

this job last year, (3) .... college. He is a

'mystery shopper', (4) .... going to shops

(5) .... and pretending to be a customer.

He talks to staff in shops, (6) .... he's

working for the company. He then writes reports

(7) .... his experience in the shops. He

describes aspects of the service (8) ....

to improve.

❸ Combine the pairs of sentences in *a* about supermarkets in Britain, using a relative clause.

1 a Tesco is one of Britain's biggest supermarket chains. It employs over 50,000 people.

  b Tesco, ...*which is one of Britain's biggest*.... ....*supermarket chains, employs*.... over 50,000 people.

2 a Tesco's profits are very high. It is one of Britain's most successful companies.

  b Tesco, ... one of one of Britain's most successful companies.

3 a In the 1980s supermarkets began to appear all over Britain. Tesco was one of the main ones.

  b In the 1980s, ... was one of the main ones.

4 a British people used to buy their food in small shops. They quickly changed to shopping in supermarkets.

  b British people, ... to shopping in supermarkets.

5 a In small towns, many small shops have closed. People go to out-of-town supermarkets instead.

  b In small towns, ... go to out-of-town supermarkets instead.

6 a Supermarkets now sell a variety of things. They are a fundamental part of the British way of life.

  b Supermarkets, ... a fundamental part of the British way of life.

Unit 7 Relationships

Listening Part 3

1 You will hear two students talking about a presentation. Look at the second task, Questions 6–10. What kind of word will be required for all of the questions? Circle A, B or C.

A adverbs **B** verbs **C** nouns

2 (08) Now listen and answer Questions 1–10.

Questions 1–5

Choose the correct letter, A, B or C.

1 Maya chose the topic of lifelong friendships because
  A it was an unusual area of research.
  B she had a particular interest in it.
  C someone suggested it to her.

2 Maya says that the sample of people she used
  A was smaller than she wanted it to be.
  B was typical of the population in general.
  C was the basis for further work.

3 The problem with the questionnaire was that
  A it wasn't well constructed.
  B the subjects couldn't engage with it.
  C too much time was required to complete it.

4 Maya says that when she conducted the interviews,
  A she kept brief notes.
  B the subjects were all very relaxed.
  C they followed a clear structure.

5 What does Maya say about other research in the area?
  A A lot of it contradicted her findings.
  B It wasn't very easy to find.
  C It was carried out in the same way as hers.

Questions 6–10

Complete the flow chart below.

*Write **NO MORE THAN TWO WORDS** for each answer.*

Lifelong friendships presentation

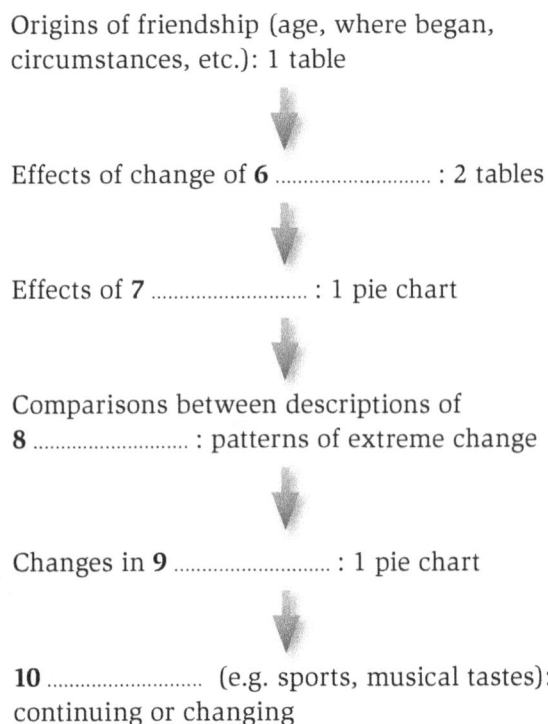

Origins of friendship (age, where began, circumstances, etc.): 1 table

⬇

Effects of change of **6** .... : 2 tables

⬇

Effects of **7** .... : 1 pie chart

⬇

Comparisons between descriptions of **8** .... : patterns of extreme change

⬇

Changes in **9** .... : 1 pie chart

⬇

10 .... (e.g. sports, musical tastes): continuing or changing

---

Vocabulary

Feelings

▶ Student's Book unit 7, p68

❶ Complete the sentences with the adjectives in the box.

bored	reassuring	upset	~~irritated~~
helpful	concerned	persuasive	
irritating	boring	upsetting	

1 I get very ....*irritated*.... when people keep asking me stupid questions.
2 She was so .... that I ended up agreeing to what she wanted.
3 I wasn't at all .... because I knew nothing bad was going to happen.
4 Donna gets .... if people criticise her and she often starts crying.
5 I was so .... at the party that I nearly fell asleep.
6 You've been very .... and I couldn't have done this without you.
7 It's .... to know that I'm not the only person with this problem.
8 It was a very .... experience and I felt bad about it for a long time.
9 The conversation was extremely .... and I stopped listening.
10 His behaviour was very .... and I shouted at him.

Age(s) / aged / age group

❷ Complete these results from a survey about social networking sites by circling the correct options in each of these sentences.

1 The highest number of people using the sites was in the 16–24 *ages* /*(age group)*.
2 35% of children started using the sites at *the age / ages* of 12 or under.
3 45% of users *ages / aged* 16–24 checked for messages every day.
4 65% of parents *aged / age* below 40 said that they looked at their children's activities on the sites.
5 5% of people over *age / the age* of 70 used the sites to keep in touch with family.

6 10% of people between *ages / the ages* of 40 and 50 used the sites regularly.
7 People of different *age / ages* used the sites for different reasons.
8 The 60+ *ages / age group* had the lowest number of users.
9 80% of users were under 30 years of *age / aged*.
10 People in the lower *age groups / ages* used the sites more than older people.

Key vocabulary

❸ Complete the sentences below, then use the words to complete this crossword.

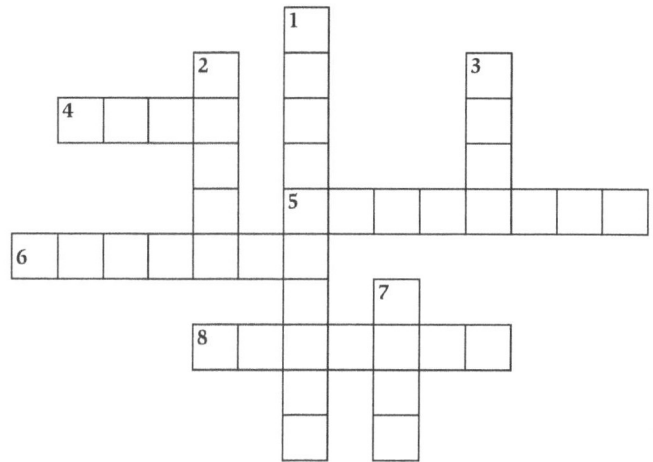

Across

4 If you can .... the difference between two things, the difference is clear to you.
5 An .... is an unusual or bad event that happens.
6 If you .... to doing something bad, you say that you did it.
8 If you .... something, you say what will happen in the future.

Down

1 If results are .... , they are the same over a period of time.
2 If you .... someone for something, you say they are responsible for something bad.
3 Animals living in the .... are living in their natural habitat, not in a zoo.
7 A .... is someone who doesn't tell the truth.

Reading Section 2

❶ **Read through the article quickly. Then look at Questions 7–10 and answer the following.**

In which sections of the text are there references to the people listed? ....

❷ **Now read the text carefully and answer Questions 1–13.**

ESTABLISHING YOUR BIRTHRIGHTS

Position in the family can play a huge role in shaping character, finds Clover Stroud

A Last week I was given a potent reminder of how powerful birth order might be in determining a child's character. My son, Jimmy Joe, nine, and my daughter, Dolly, six, were re-enacting a TV talent show. Jimmy Joe elected himself judge and Dolly was a contestant. Authoritative and unyielding, he wielded a clipboard, delivering harsh criticisms that would make a real talent show judge flinch. Initially Dolly loved the attention, but she soon grew tired of his dominance, instigating a pillow fight, then a fist fight. It ended, inevitably, in tears. A visiting friend, with an older, more successful sister, declared it 'classic first child behaviour of dominance and supposed authority'. Dolly's objection to her brother's self-appointed role as leader was justified, he announced, while Jimmy Joe's superiority was characteristic of the forceful personality of firstborns. Birth order, he said, wasn't something they could just shrug off.

B Debate about the significance of birth order goes right to the heart of the nature versus nurture argument and is, consequently, surrounded by huge controversy. This controversy has raged since the 19th century, when Austrian psychiatrist Alfred Adler argued that birth order can define the way someone deals with life. He identified firstborns as driven and often suffering from a sense of having been 'dethroned' by a second child. Younger children, he stated, were hampered by having been more pampered than older siblings. It's a view reiterated by Professor Frank Sulloway's influential work, *Born to Rebel*. Sulloway, a leading proponent of the birth-order idea, argued it has a definitive effect on the 'Big Five' personality traits of openness, conscientiousness, extroversion, agreeableness and neuroticism.

C According to the birth-order theory, first children are usually well-organised high achievers. However, they can have an overdeveloped sense of entitlement and be unyielding. Second children are sometimes very competitive through rivalry with the older sibling. They're also good mediators and negotiators, keen to keep everyone happy. Middle children, tagged the 'easy' ones, have good diplomacy skills. They suffer from a tendency to feel insignificant beside other siblings and often complain of feeling invisible to their parents. Youngest children are often the most likely to rebel, feeling the need to 'prove' themselves. They're often extroverts and are sometimes accused of being selfish. Twins inevitably find it harder to see themselves as individuals, unless their parents have worked hard to identify them as such. It's not unusual for one twin to have a slightly dominant role over the other and take the lead role.

D But slapping generalised labels on a child is dangerous; they change all the time, often taking turns at being the 'naughty one' or the 'diligent one'. However, as one of five children, I know how hard it is to transcend the tags you earn according to when you were born. It is unsurprising then that my eldest sister is the successful entrepreneur, and that, despite covering all the big bases of adult life like marriage, kids and property, my siblings will probably always regard me as their spoilt younger sister.

E 'As the oldest of three, I've found it hard not to think of my own three children as having the same personality types that the three of us had when I was growing up,' says Lisa Cannan, a teacher. 'I identify with my eldest son, who constantly takes the lead in terms of organisation and responsibility. My daughter, the middle child, is more cerebral than her brothers. She's been easier than them. She avoids confrontation, so has an easy relationship with both boys. My youngest is gorgeous but naughty. I know I'm partly to blame for this, as I forgive him things the elder two wouldn't get away with.'

F As a parent, it's easy to feel guilty about saddling a child with labels according to birth order, but as child psychologist Stephen Bayliss points out, these characteristics might be better attributed to parenting styles, rather than a child's character. He says that if a parent is worried about having encouraged, for example, an overdeveloped sense of dominance in an older sibling or spoiled a younger child, then it's more useful to look at ways this can be addressed than over-analysing why it happened. Bayliss is optimistic that as adults we can overcome any negative connotations around birth order. 'Look at the way you react to certain situations with your siblings. If you're unhappy about being treated as a certain type of personality, try to work out if it's a role that you've willingly accepted. If you're unhappy with the role, being dynamic about focusing on your own reactions, rather than blaming theirs, will help you overcome it. Change isn't easy but nobody need be the victim of their biography.'

Questions 1–6

The reading passage has six paragraphs, **A–F**.

Choose the correct heading for each paragraph from the list of headings below.

> i Children's views on birth order
> ii Solutions are more important than causes
> iii Characteristics common to all children regardless of birth order
> iv Doubts about birth-order theory but personal experience supporting it
> v A theory that is still supported
> vi Birth-order characteristics continuing as children get older
> vii A typical example of birth-order behaviour in practice
> viii Exceptions to the rule of birth order
> ix A detailed description of each child in families in general

1 Paragraph A ....
2 Paragraph B ....
3 Paragraph C ....
4 Paragraph D ....
5 Paragraph E ....
6 Paragraph F ....

Questions 7–10

Look at the following statements (Questions 7–10) and the list of people below.

*Match each statement with the correct person, **A–D**.*

You may use any letter more than once.

7 Experience as a child can affect behaviour as a parent.
8 Birth order may not be the main reason why children have the personalities they have.
9 There is a link between birth and a group of important characteristics.
10 It is possible for people to stop feeling bad about how family members behave with them.

List of people

A Alfred Adler
B Professor Frank Sulloway
C Lisa Cannan
D Stephen Bayliss

Questions 11–13

Complete the sentences below.

*Choose **ONE WORD ONLY** from the passage for each answer.*

11 First-born children have expectations that are too high with regard to ....
12 Middle children are often considered .... by their parents.
13 Youngest children may be described as .... by other people.

Writing Task 1

❶ **Look at the Writing task below. Which is the best title for the two pie charts? Circle A, B or C.**

A Happiness of parents before and after having children

B Happiness of parents compared with happiness of children

C Happiness of parents with children of different ages

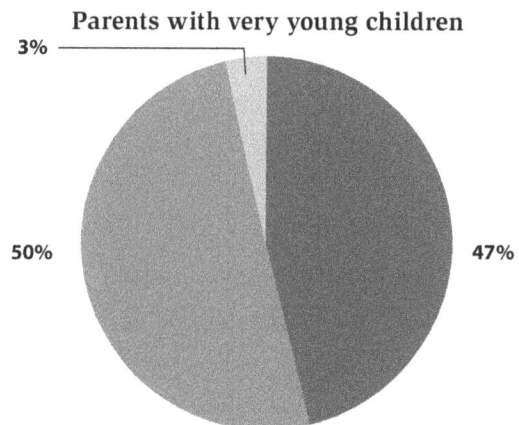

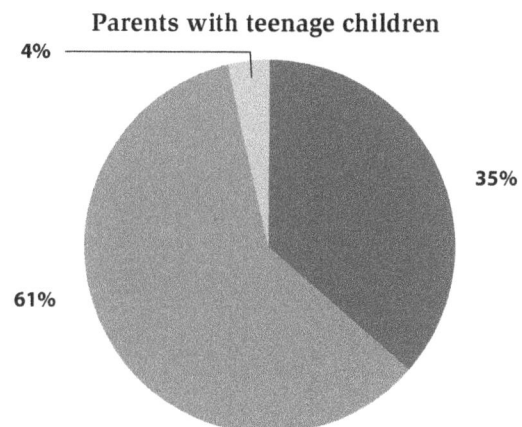

Parents with very young children

3%
50%
47%

Parents with teenage children

4%
61%
35%

■ Very happy ■ Fairly happy ■ Unhappy

2 Which of the following are main differences between the two charts? Write *Yes* or *No*.

A the categories in the charts ....

B the percentages of very happy people ....

C the percentages of fairly happy people ....

D the percentages of unhappy people ....

E the ages of children ....

F the totals of very happy and fairly happy people ....

3 Which of the following overviews is the best? Circle A, B or C.

A The main conclusion from the pie charts is that parents with very young children were happy but parents with older children were not.

B In general, parents got happier as their children got older.

C To sum up, parents with teenage children were less happy than parents with very young children, but very few of them were unhappy.

4 Look at the Writing task on the right. What are the main features of the charts? Write *Yes* or *No*.

A differences between the two years ....

B how high certain figures are ....

C similarities between the two relationships ....

D how many people couldn't answer ....

E differences in the two relationships ....

F how much certain figures fell ....

G similarities between the two years ....

H how low certain figures are ....

The charts below show the results of surveys in 2005 and 2009 asking workers about their relationships with their supervisors and their co-workers.

Summarise the information by reporting the main features, and make comparisons where relevant.

**Relationships at work
(survey of workers 2005 & 2009)**

Relationships with supervisor

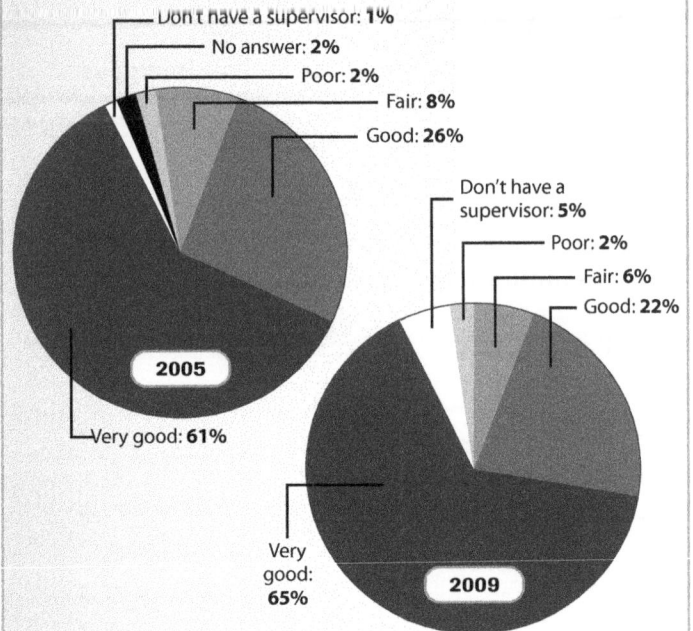

Don't have a supervisor: 1%
No answer: 2%
Poor: 2%
Fair: 8%
Good: 26%

2005

Very good: 61%

Don't have a supervisor: 5%
Poor: 2%
Fair: 6%
Good: 22%

Very good: 65%

2009

Relationships with co-workers

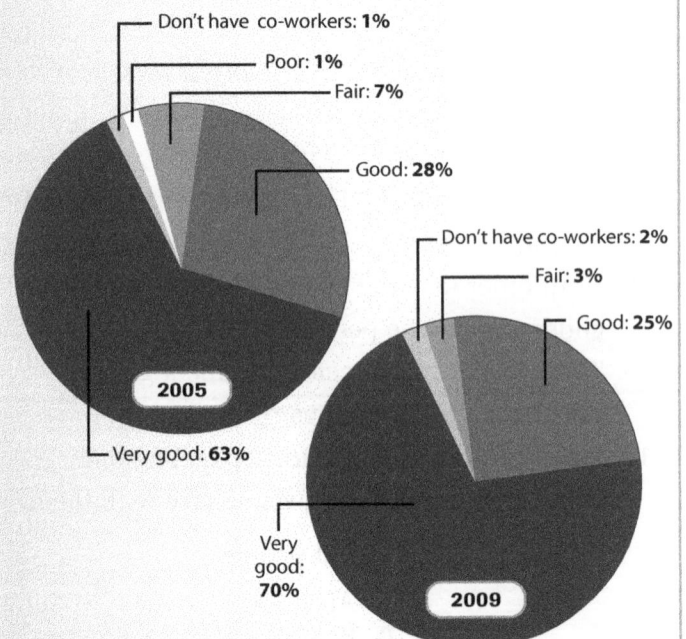

Don't have co-workers: 1%
Poor: 1%
Fair: 7%
Good: 28%

2005

Very good: 63%

Don't have co-workers: 2%
Fair: 3%
Good: 25%

Very good: 70%

2009

5 Now write your answer for the Writing task above.

Grammar

Reference devices

▶ Student's Book unit 7, p75

❶ **Complete this text about self-help books with the correct reference devices, for example, *them, it, this, one, other*, etc.**

Self-help books about relationships have been very popular for some years and **(1)** ...they... sell in very large quantities. But why do people use **(2)** .... ? Why are **(3)** .... books so popular?

(4) .... kind of book is the kind that tells people how to improve **(5)** .... relationships with **(6)** .... people in **(7)** .... personal lives. According to research, women often buy **(8)** .... kind of self-help book. **(9)** .... books give advice about relationships with your boyfriend or husband and a woman might buy **(10)** .... of them because **(11)** .... thinks that **(12)** .... will give her good ideas on how to deal with **(13)** .... person.

Another kind of self-help book deals with how to be successful in life by having good relationships at work. Some of the most successful **(14)** .... in this category are about relationships in the workplace, and according to research, **(15)** .... is a subject that appeals to men more than women. A man might buy a book in **(16)** .... category because **(17)** .... believes **(18)** .... claims that **(19)** .... will help **(20)** .... to rise to the top and make lots of money.

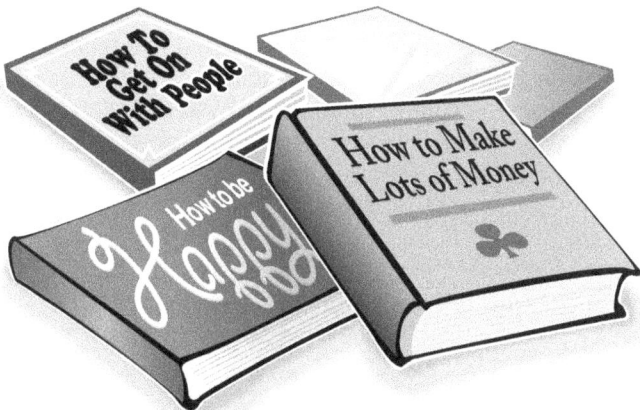

Zero, first and second conditionals

❷ **Correct the underlined phrases in these sentences if necessary. Put a tick (✓) above them if they are correct.**

                                    he'd make
1 If Harry was more pleasant to people, <u>he'll make</u> more friends.

2 If <u>you'll get on</u> well with your boss, work is enjoyable.

3 People don't enjoy life <u>unless they have</u> good relationships with other people.

4 I don't argue with my friends unless <u>they would upset</u> me.

5 If we discuss this calmly, <u>we won't have</u> an argument.

6 If <u>I wouldn't like</u> him, I wouldn't accept his bad behaviour towards me.

7 If you need some help tomorrow, <u>I give</u> it to you.

8 Unless <u>you apologise</u>, he'll be very angry with you.

9 <u>I'll be</u> unhappy if I didn't have my friends to go out with.

10 If I didn't trust Tara, <u>I wouldn't tell</u> her my secrets.

11 We don't go to that restaurant unless it <u>will be</u> my birthday.

12 I'd live in this town forever if I <u>had</u> the choice.

13 If I were you, I <u>won't</u> marry him.

14 If I <u>don't phone</u> my grandmother every Sunday, she gets very upset.

15 I'd be fitter if I <u>exercise</u> more.

Unit 8 Fashion and design

Reading Section 3

❶ Read through the article about fashion briefly. Then look at Questions 11–14 and answer the following.

What is the best way of answering these questions? Circle A, B or C.

A by finding the people mentioned in the questions

B by finding the ideas mentioned in the options

C by reading the whole text again

❷ Now read the text carefully and answer Questions 1–14.

MAKING A LOSS IS THE HEIGHT OF FASHION

In this topsy-turvy world, selling a dress at an enormous discount turns out to be very good business indeed, says William Langley

Given that a good year in the haute couture business is one where you lose even more money than usual, the prevailing mood in Paris last week was of buoyancy. The big-name designers were falling over themselves to boast of how many outfits they had sold at below cost price, and how this proved that the fashion business was healthier than ever. Jean-Paul Gaultier reported record sales, "but we don't make any money out of it," the designer assured journalists backstage. "No matter how successful you are, you can't make a profit from couture," explained Jean-Jacques Picart, a veteran fashion PR man, and co-founder of the now-bankrupt Lacroix house.

Almost 20 years have passed since the bizarre economics of the couture business were first exposed. Outraged that he was losing money on evening dresses costing tens of thousands of pounds, the couturier Jean-Louis Scherrer – to howls of "treason" from his colleagues – published a detailed summary of his costs. One outfit he described contained over half a mile of gold thread, 18,000 sequins, and had required hundreds of hours of hand-stitching in an atelier. A fair price would have been £50,000, but the couturier could only get £35,000 for it. Rather than riding high on the follies of the super-rich, he and his team could barely feed their hungry families.

The result was an outcry and the first of a series of government- and industry-sponsored inquiries into the surreal world of ultimate fashion. The trade continues to insist that – relatively speaking – couture offers you more than you pay for, but it's not as simple as that. When such a temple of old wealth starts talking about value for money, it isn't to convince anyone that dresses costing as much as houses are a bargain. Rather, it is to preserve the peculiar mystique, lucrative associations and threatened interests that couture represents.

Essentially, the arguments couldn't be simpler. On one side are those who say that the business will die if it doesn't change. On the other are those who say it will die if it does. What's not in doubt is that haute couture – the term translates as "high sewing" – is a spectacular anachronism. Colossal in its costs, tiny in its clientele and questionable in its influence, it still remains one of the great themes of Parisian life. In his book, *The Fashion Conspiracy*, Nicholas Coleridge estimates that the entire couture industry rests on the whims of less than 30 immensely wealthy women, and although the number may have grown in recent years with the new prosperity of Asia, the number of couture customers worldwide is no more than 4,000.

To qualify as couture, a garment must be entirely hand-made by one of the 11 Paris couture houses registered to the Chambre Syndicale de la Haute Couture. Each house must employ at least 20 people, and show a minimum of 75 new designs a year. So far, so traditional, but the Big Four operators – Chanel, Dior, Givenchy and Gaultier – increasingly use couture as a marketing device for their far more profitable ready-to-wear, fragrance and accessory lines.

It isn't hard to see how this works in practice. "Haute couture is what gives our business its essential essence of luxury," says Bernard Arnault, the head of LVMH, which

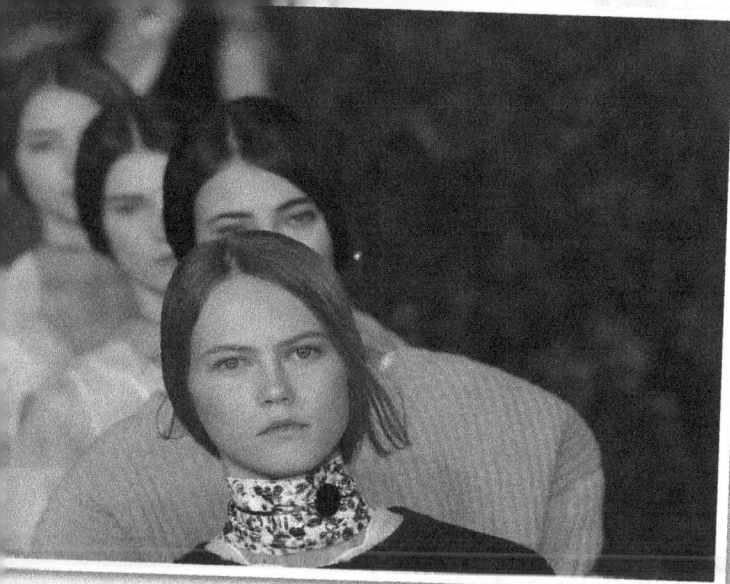

owns both Dior and Givenchy. "The cash it soaks up is largely irrelevant. Set against the money we lose has to be the value of the image couture gives us. Look at the attention the collections attract. It is where you get noticed. You have to be there. It's where we set our ideas in motion."

The big idea being the one known in the trade as "name association". Couture outfits may be unaffordable, even unwearable, but the whiff of glamour and exclusivity is hard to resist. The time-starved modern woman who doesn't make enough in a year to afford a single piece of couture can still buy a share of the dream for the price of a Chanel lipstick or a Givenchy scarf.

For all this, couture has been in decline – the optimists would say readjusting to changed conditions – for years. The number of houses registered to the Syndicale has halved in the last two decades. Pierre Cardin once had almost 500 people working full time on couture, but by the 1980s the number had fallen to 50, and today the house is no longer registered.

Modern life tells the story. Younger women, even the seriously wealthy ones, find ready-to-wear clothes invariably more practical and usually more fun. Couture's market has dwindled. "Haute couture is a joke," scoffs Pierre Bergé, the former head of Yves St Laurent – another house that no longer creates it. "Anyone who tells you it still matters is fantasising. You can see it dropping dead all around you. Nobody buys it any more. The prices are ridiculous. The rules for making it are nonsensical. It belongs to another age. Where are today's couturiers? A real couturier is someone who founds and runs their own house. No one does that any more."

Why, then, are the surviving couture houses smiling? Because they trade in fantasy, and, in these times, more people want to fantasise. "We've received so many orders we may not be able to deliver them all," says Sidney Toledano, head of Dior. So, the clothes are rolled out and the couture losses roll in, and everyone agrees that it's good business.

Questions 1–5

*Choose the correct letter, **A**, **B**, **C** or **D**.*

1 What is the main topic of the first paragraph?
   A the difference between haute couture and other areas of the fashion industry
   B contrasting views on haute couture
   C the losses made on haute couture
   D the negative attitude towards haute couture of people in the fashion industry

2 The writer says that Jean-Louis Scherrer
   A upset other couturiers.
   B was in a worse financial position than other couturiers.
   C was one of the best-known couturiers.
   D stopped producing haute couture dresses.

3 The writer says that the outfit Jean-Louis Scherrer described
   A was worth the price that was paid for it.
   B cost more to make than it should have.
   C was never sold to anyone.
   D should have cost more to buy than it did.

4 In the third paragraph, the writer states that haute couture makers
   A think that the term 'value for money' has a particular meaning for them.
   B prefer to keep quiet about the financial aspects of the business.
   C have changed because of inquiries into how they operate.
   D want to expand their activities to attract new customers.

5 The writer says in the fourth paragraph that there is disagreement over
   A the popularity of haute couture.
   B the future of haute couture.
   C the real costs of haute couture.
   D the changes that need to be made in haute couture.

Questions 6–10

Do the following statements agree with the views of the writer in the reading passage?

Write

YES   *if the statement agrees with the views of the writer*

NO   *if the statement contradicts the views of the writer*

NOT GIVEN   *if it is impossible to say what the writer thinks about this*

6 The way that companies use haute couture as a marketing device is clear.

7 Only wealthy people are attracted by the idea of 'name association'.

8 Pierre Cardin is likely to return to producing haute couture.

9 Some women who can afford haute couture clothes buy other clothes instead.

10 It is hard to understand why some haute couture companies are doing well.

Questions 11–14

Complete each sentence with the correct ending, A–F, below.

11 In his book, Nicholas Coleridge claims that

12 The head of LVMH believes that

13 The former head of Yves St Laurent feels that

14 The head of Dior states that

A there is great demand for haute couture.
B people who defend haute couture are wrong.
C the cost of haute couture is likely to come down.
D haute couture is dependent on a very small number of customers.
E more companies will start producing haute couture.
F it is important to continue with haute couture.

Listening Part 4

❶ You will hear part of a lecture about jeans.
Look at Questions 1–10.
What is the main focus of the task? Circle A, B or C.

A developments connected with jeans

B the different uses of jeans

C attitudes towards jeans

❷ (09) Now listen and answer Questions 1–10.

Questions 1–10

Complete the sentences below.

*Write **NO MORE THAN TWO WORDS** for each answer.*

1 The word jeans may have originated in a material used in clothes worn by .... from Italy.

2 One difference between jean and denim material concerned the .... used to create them.

3 Denim was used in the clothes worn by people whose place of work was ....

4 Strauss's first name was originally

....

5 The miners' problem concerned the .... on their clothes.

6 Strauss's clothes solved the problem because they used .... fasteners.

7 The label Strauss added showed his waist overalls connected to ....

8 In the 1930s, the clothes became more popular because people saw characters in .... wearing them.

9 In the 1940s, people in other countries saw the clothes being worn by .... from the U.S.

10 In the 1950s, teenagers called the clothes

....

Vocabulary

Dress (uncountable) / *dresses* (countable) / *clothes* / *cloth*

❶ **Circle the correct option in each of these sentences.**

1 My grandmother made my *clothes / cloth* when I was a child. She always cut the *clothes / cloth* very carefully.
2 *Dress / Dresses* for this event will be informal.
3 She doesn't have great interest in *clothes / dress* and fashion in general.
4 She didn't take enough *dress / dresses* on the trip with her.
5 The teacher got some *cloth / dress* and showed the children how to make a rabbit from it.
6 The weather isn't warm enough for summer *cloth / dresses*.

Key vocabulary

❷ **Complete the sentences below, then use the words to complete this crossword.**

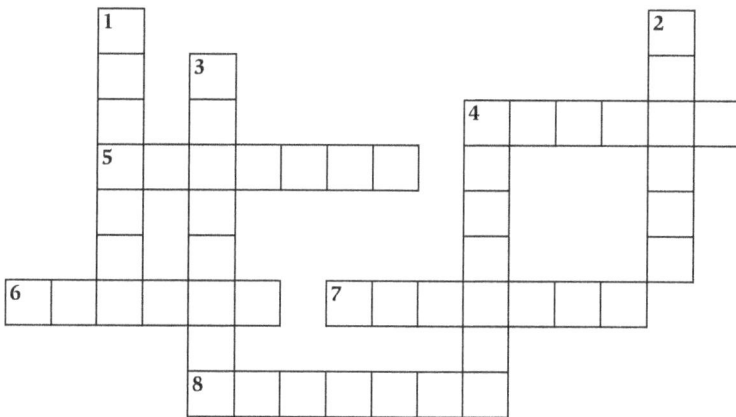

Across

4 A .... is a kind of material or cloth.
5 A .... is an item of clothing.
6 .... clothes are informal.
7 If something is .... , it is very very old.
8 A .... is a kind of cloth made by weaving.

Down

1 The .... of something are how it started.
2 If something is .... , there is nothing like it.
3 A .... is a picture of a person, especially the person's head/face.
4 If something is .... , it might easily break and must be treated carefully.

❸ **Complete the sentences below with the words in the box. There are two words which do not fit into any of the gaps.**

celebrity	functional
conservation	performance
decorative	~~repair~~
contemporary	retire
produced	preserve

1 This jumper has a very big hole in it and you won't be able to ......*repair*...... it.
2 During her fashion course, she compared .... clothes with clothes from the past.
3 The best way to .... these clothes is to keep them out of the light.
4 These clothes are all .... by hand and that's why they take a long time to make.
5 She always wanted to be famous and attract attention from the media, so she was very happy when she became a ....
6 These clothes are very .... and can be worn both for work and social occasions.
7 He gave a wonderful .... in the film and the critics said he was a brilliant actor.
8 The clothes made by this company have a .... design on the front of them.

Writing Task 2

❶ Read the following Writing task.

Write about the following topic:

Some people say that the clothes people wear are the most important indication of what they are like. Others, however, say that people should not be judged by the clothes they wear.

Discuss both these views and give your own opinion.

Give reasons for your answer and include any relevant examples from your knowledge or experience.

Below are three essay plans that candidates made for this question. Which two of the essay plans are suitable? Why are they suitable and why is the other essay plan not suitable?

A

Paragraph 1: introduction – importance of the latest fashions to people today, especially the young

Paragraph 2: why people want to follow the latest fashions – celebrities, advertising, etc.

Paragraph 3: result – people all over the world wearing the same clothes, loss of national identity through wearing of different clothes

Paragraph 4: conclusion – people shouldn't copy each other's clothes, should express their own individuality through what they wear

B

Paragraph 1: introduction – people often judge others by the clothes they wear + example

Paragraph 2: examples of when it is right to judge people by the clothes they wear, e.g. at work

Paragraph 3: other things that indicate what people are like – not clothes but behaviour, the way they speak, etc.

Paragraph 4: conclusion – why it's not always right to judge people by the clothes they wear

C

Paragraph 1: introduction – people who wear clothes to impress others / people who don't do this

Paragraph 2: importance of clothes worn for work – the impression they give

Paragraph 3: clothes not worn at work – fashions among the young and the impression they want to give

Paragraph 4: my opinion: clothes for work and impression they give important, outside work not important and can't judge people from what they wear

❷ What *must* you mention in your answer? Write *Yes* or *No*.

A   a contrast between past and present attitudes to clothes   ....

B   the connection between clothes and opinions of people   ....

C   current fashions in clothes   ....

D   contrasting views on the importance of clothes   ....

E   clothes worn by famous people   ....

F   a personal view on the importance of clothes   ....

G   clothes worn in different parts of the world   ....

H   the kind of clothes you like to wear   ....

❸ Which of these candidate's notes about topic areas for the answer are relevant to the task and which are not? Write *Yes* or *No*.

A   more important things than clothes   ....

B   clothes and advertising   ....

C   teenage fashions   ....

D   when clothes are important   ....

E   cost of fashionable clothes   ....

F   clothes and image   ....

G   work clothes   ....

H   how fashions start   ....

❹ Now write your answer for the Writing task above.

Grammar

Time conjunctions: *until/before/when/after*

❶ Make sentences by matching 1–6 with A–F.

1 I want to buy a new coat
2 I can't wear that shirt again
3 I'm going to get changed
4 I'll decide whether to buy this or not
5 I can wear this jumper again
6 I'm not going to buy a new suit

A until I really need one.
B before I go out.
C when I find one I really like.
D when I've repaired it.
E after I've tried it on.
F until I've washed it.

❷ Correct the <u>underlined</u> words if necessary. Put a tick (✓) above the words if they are correct.

1 Make sure it suits you before <u>you'll buy</u> it. *you buy*

2 She won't be happy until <u>she's found</u> something new to wear.

3 When <u>I go</u> shopping I don't like trying on lots of clothes.

4 When <u>people will get</u> a bit older, they change the kind of clothes they wear.

5 After <u>I've bought</u> some new trousers, I'm going to go home.

6 When <u>I've paid</u> for these clothes, I won't have any money left.

7 I'm going to keep looking until <u>I'm finding</u> something I like.

8 You should repair the jumper before that hole <u>will get</u> bigger.

9 When <u>I've got</u> changed, I'll be ready to go out.

10 I won't buy any clothes until <u>I tried</u> them on.

❸ Complete the sentences below with the words in the box.

I get	I've worn	I've chosen	I wash	I've had
I've found	I'm	~~I've saved~~	I leave	I throw

1 I won't be able to buy that dress until ...I've saved... some money.
2 When .... college, I'll have to buy some smart clothes for work.
3 After .... which shirt to wear, I'll get ready to go out.
4 When .... a shower, I'll put on my new clothes.
5 I'll buy some new swimming trunks when .... on holiday.
6 These new shoes will feel more comfortable when .... them a few times.
7 Before .... these jeans away, I'll try to repair them.
8 When .... the receipt, I'll take these clothes back to the shop.
9 I won't wear this suit again until .... married next month.
10 I'll check the instructions before .... this jumper in the machine.

Recording script

Unit 1

Track 2

You will hear an interviewer asking a member of the public for his views on the city.

First you have some time to look at Questions 1–5. You will see that there is an example that has been done for you. On this occasion only, the conversation relating to this will be played first.

Interviewer Hello, we're conducting a survey about what people think of this city. I wonder, would you mind answering a few questions?

Man I'm in a bit of a hurry.

I Well, it won't take long, just a couple of minutes of your time …

M Well, OK, but I haven't been living here for long, so I might not be able to answer some of your questions.

I That's not a problem, we're looking for views from a range of people. Could I just get a few details first?

M OK, I guess.

I Well, first of all, which age group do you fit into? 18 to 24, 25 to 34, 35 to 50?

M I'm 28, so that's the middle one of those, what was it, 25 to 34?

I Yes.

M OK, that's me.

The man is aged 28 and in the 25 to 34 age group, so 25 to 34 has been written in the space.

Now we shall begin. You should answer the questions as you listen as you will not hear the recording a second time.

I Hello, we're conducting a survey about what people think of this city. I wonder, would you mind answering a few questions?

M I'm in a bit of a hurry.

I Well, it won't take long, just a couple of minutes of your time …

M Well, OK, but I haven't been living here for long, so I might not be able to answer some of your questions.

I That's not a problem, we're looking for views from a range of people. Could I just get a few details first?

M OK, I guess.

I Well, first of all, which age group do you fit into? 18 to 24, 25 to 34, 35 to 50.

M I'm 28, so that's the middle one of those, what was it, 25 to 34?

I Yes.

M OK, that's me.

I And how long have you been living in this city?

M I've only been here for three weeks and it's my first experience of this country at all. I've come here to work on a six-month contract.

I Right, so it's all pretty new for you?

M Yes, I'm still getting used to it.

I Right. So, where did you live previously?

M I'm from New Zealand. I lived there all my life before I came to Britain.

I Oh, really? I haven't met anybody else from your country before.

M No? Well, there are a few of us here.

I OK, perhaps I'll meet some more while I'm doing this. Now, the next question is 'occupation' – did you say you came here for work?

M Yes, that's right. I'm a lawyer. My firm has sent me here to gain some experience of practising law in an international context. So, I'm here to learn really.

I Sounds very interesting.

M Yes, I'm already learning a lot. Things are very different here from back at home.

I Now, what area of the city are you living in?

M I'm in an apartment in Waterfall Road, that's in Coundon.

I Oh, OK, let's see, how's that spelt, C-O-U-N-D-O-N, that's right, isn't it? It's O-N at the end, not E-N, isn't it?

M Yes, that's right.

I And your postcode, if you can remember it. Just the first part will do.

M That's CV26.

I OK, thanks.

Pause

I Now I want to ask you for your views on various aspects of living here. First of all, public transport. Is the public transport system adequate for you?

M Mm, well, it's hard to say. When I've used it, it's been fine, but I don't use it all that often. I cycle to work every day and that's usually how I get around in my free time, too. So, I'm not sure I can comment really on that particular issue.

I No improvements to suggest then?

M No, I don't have enough experience to do that.

I OK, now sports facilities. Do you do much sport?

M Yes, I do, it's my main interest outside work and I've got no criticisms there. As soon as I arrived I joined a cricket club – a friend back home who'd lived here for a while told me about it – and I've made lots of friends there already.

I Apart from that, do you think there are enough facilities?

M Yes, as far as I can see. I use the public swimming pool regularly, I've found some very good tennis courts and the fitness centre is fine, too. I've been able to carry on doing all the sports I'm used to doing at home.

I What about entertainment? Is this adequately provided or is the city lacking in something?

M Well, coming from a pretty small town, I've been amazed at what's on offer here. There are so many things to choose from in the evenings and at weekends. I don't think I'll have time to go everywhere I'd like to while I'm here. I've already been to some excellent restaurants, I've been to the cinema a few times, I've been to all sorts of places. There seem to be loads of things to do.

I What about cleanliness and litter? Do you have any views on that?

M Well, to be honest, I've been pretty surprised about that. Before I came, for some reason I'd had the impression that it would be a pretty dirty place, certainly compared with where I'm from. You know, I was expecting a crowded city with litter and rubbish all over the place, and sure there is some litter and it could all be a bit cleaner, but actually It's not at all bad in that respect.

I OK, now, what about crime and the police force? What are your views on that aspect of life in this city?

M Well, I haven't been here long enough to form much of a view. A colleague at work had her car broken into and some things stolen, and she reported it to the police but there wasn't much they could do about it, apart from give her a crime number so that she could claim on her insurance. I don't know how common that sort of thing is here. Nothing's happened to me so far, that's all I can say. Perhaps I've just been lucky or perhaps crime isn't a major problem, I don't know. But there's crime everywhere, isn't there, all over the world and in the countryside as well as cities.

I OK, well I've got all the information I need for the survey and I've ticked the right boxes. Thanks for taking the time to answer the questions.

M No problem.

Unit 2

Track 3

You will hear a speaker introducing a conference. First, you have some time to look at Questions 1–10.

Pause

Now listen and answer Questions 1–10.

Hello, and welcome to the conference. As you know, it's called Health & Fitness in the Workplace, and the name speaks for itself. We're here to discuss issues that can affect employees and of course therefore, the companies and organisations they work for. In planning the programme for this conference, we've taken into account the answers that you gave us in our questionnaires. Of course, some of the issues we cover will be more relevant to some of you than to others, but we think we've included all the main ones that you indicated are important to you.

Now, the whole subject of health and fitness in the workplace is something that didn't get much attention not that many years ago. Companies and organisations focused purely on the jobs that people were doing, and any assessment of them concerned how well they were doing their jobs, and how their work fitted into the overall operations of the organisation. Anything that might be regarded as a personal issue wasn't part of the company's relationship with its people – it was 'none of their business'. Well, of course, that's all changed and companies and organisations have come to realise that its people's health and fitness are very much their business. And that's not just in the obvious ways, such as the number of days off sick that employees have. There are also

psychological factors, and there is considerable evidence that a fit and healthy person does their job better than someone who doesn't maintain a good level of health and fitness. If you're emphasising these things at your workplace, you're creating an atmosphere that enables you to get the very best out of your people.

We're very much hoping that our programme here at the conference will be both informative and entertaining. The emphasis here is going to be not so much on the theory but on the practical side. What can you do in your roles to promote health and fitness in your workplace? Now, some of you may think you're already doing as much as you can, but I promise you that you're all going to learn something new. We've got speakers here who are going to tell you things you've never heard before and you should leave here at the end of the conference with all kinds of ideas for things you can introduce at your workplace.

But we're not going to be just talking to you and telling you things. One of the great things about an event like this is that it's a great opportunity to share information, so in every session there will be a slot for people to talk about their own practices and experiences. What initiatives have worked for you and which ones haven't been so successful? We can all learn from each other, and that's one of the aims of this conference.

Pause

OK, now let's move on to some details about the conference and what will be happening where. Let me just briefly take you through the map that you've all got in your welcome pack. Right, here on the map, we've marked all the sessions that are taking place this morning, and you've already indicated which ones you'll each be attending. For those of you going to the session on Setting Up a Fitness Centre at work, you go out of the Main Hall here through those doors, turn right at reception and go along the corridor to the Taylor Room, which is on your left. You'll get lots of good advice there on the possibilities and costs of a workplace fitness centre.

The talk on Healthy Eating Schemes is in the Martin Suite. For that, you need to go out of this hall the other way, through the doors at that end, and that takes you straight through to the Martin Suite. If you're keen to introduce healthy eating schemes in your canteens and restaurants, or to improve ones you've already got, you'll get lots of really good ideas from that session.

Now, those of you attending the session on Transport Initiatives, you're in the Fender Room. To get there, you need to go out of those doors that bring you out opposite reception, turn left and left again into a corridor. The Fender Room is the third door on your right. The session will cover everything from how to encourage people to walk or cycle to work to car-sharing schemes.

For those of you who have signed up for the workshop on Running Sports Teams, that will take place in the Gibson Suite. The whole issue of organising company teams, recruiting people for them, encouraging people to take part in them whatever their sporting ability, taking part in competitions – all that will get covered in the workshop. You'll find that if you go out of here, turn right at reception and then right again. The first door you come to on the left is the Gibson Suite.

Finally, if you need any more information or have any queries while the conference is going on, you'll find me in the Conference Coordinator's Office. From here, that's to the left of Reception and along the corridor past the Entrance Hall. If you keep going along the corridor, you'll find my door at the end on your right. Please come and see me if there's anything you want to ask or find out.

OK, let's get started. I hope that you all enjoy …

Unit 3

Track 4

You will hear a student talking to her tutor about a piece of work she has done. First, you have some time to look at Questions 1–10.

Pause

Now listen and answer Questions 1–10.

Tutor Right, Beth, let's have a look at your dissertation. Well, I think it's a pretty good piece of work.

Beth Thanks.

T Communication Skills in the Workplace. Good choice of topic.

B Thanks.

T Now, I see that you decided to focus on certain sectors ...

B Yes, I felt that jobs involving interaction with the public would be my main area. So obviously, the retail sector had to be in there ...

T Sure. But you didn't just focus on the obvious ones like that, did you?

B No, I wanted to look at a variety of sectors. I felt, for example, that banking would probably lead to the same sort of results as retail.

T And what about call centres?

B Yes, of course that seemed like an obvious place to go initially. But I decided to spread the focus away from interactions involving customers and the goods and services they buy.

T Seems sensible. So, that led you to the idea of tourist guides ...

B Yes, that's a very specific area of communication, dealing with different nationalities ...

T The skills involved in that are very interesting, as you describe them ...

B Yes, and that led me to think about the work of translators and interpreters ...

T Well, that might be the starting point for a whole other piece of work.

B Yes.

T Now, the research you did for this was generally very impressive ...

B Thanks.

T ... though a bit more on the academic research that's been done into this area would have been good.

B Well, I went more for a 'personal' approach here, rather than rehashing other people's work or focusing mainly on the theories about how people communicate.

T Yes, and it worked well. It would have been good if you could have filmed people in action and then analysed the videos.

B I know, but there were practical issues there. So I settled for watching people in action and making notes on what they were doing, and of course there were the interviews too.

T Yes, it's very interesting to compare what people think they're doing with the way they're actually communicating. I was very struck by that aspect. And your analysis from watching people in action was very effective, too.

B I found it fascinating to do that.

T Yes, that comes across. It would be fascinating to get data on the outcomes of these interactions too, whether the desired outcomes were achieved.

B I know and that would be something I'd love to look at if I knew how to go about it.

Pause

T Now, looking at the content of your dissertation, I felt your division into sections was the right one, focusing on specific types of interaction in these contexts.

B Thanks.

T Now, your first section is on Dealing with Complaints. This is an obvious area for something on this subject, but I felt that this section had some really original thinking on your part.

B Yes, I tried to ignore the standard points that are usually made and come up with something fresh, and my research led me in those directions.

T The Collaborating with Colleagues section made for interesting reading too, but I didn't feel that your conclusions there were really backed up by the research you did.

B Oh? I felt that they were. I tried to illustrate everything with examples. Perhaps some weren't as relevant as others ...

T Yes, I think that's right. You made some pretty strong assertions but I wasn't sure they could be justified by the examples.

B Oh, OK. But the evidence for my conclusions in the Interacting with Managers section was pretty powerful, wasn't it?

T Yes, and most of the research in this general area doesn't focus on this particular issue. I think your conclusions there point to something that causes all sorts of trouble in organisations and companies but that isn't given enough attention.

B I agree. It's something that training programmes should be covering, but they don't.

T Now the Giving Instructions section was very well put together, I thought ...

B Yes, this is one where language accuracy and coherence are the main issues ...

T ... and you came to very clear conclusions on that. This is a really effective section, with general points illustrated by lots of examples and a conclusion that made logical sense.

Pause

T Now, finally, let's have a quick look at your overall conclusions.

B OK.

T Now, you've included quite a bit in the main body about Writing Skills but in fact you see Listening Skills as being a much bigger issue.

B Yes, as I say there, people don't pay enough attention to what other people say to them and this leads to all kinds of communication problems.

T And the other big issue is Grammatical Accuracy, isn't it?

B Well, up to a point, but as I say, there are lots of instances where this is less of an issue than Formal Language. When people are in situations where this is required, they're often at a loss and end up not making much sense.

T Yes, as you make clear. Well, Beth, this is a good piece of work. Well done.

B Thanks.

Unit 4

Track 5

You will hear an expert giving a talk about blogs and blogging. First, you have some time to look at Questions 1–10.

Pause

Now listen and answer Questions 1–10.

OK, I'm going to talk today about blogs and blogging. Though I'm assuming you're all familiar with what a blog is, let's just start with a definition. Perhaps the simplest definition is that a blog is a type of website in the form of a journal of one sort or another. It consists of posts – new material, or entries – that are arranged in chronological order, with the most recent post at the top of the page.

Now, what are the typical characteristics of a blog? Well, blogs are usually written by one person, they are usually updated regularly and they are often, though by no means always, about one particular topic. That topic might be the blogger's own life, as many blogs are personal diaries. But there are blogs on just about any topic you could think of – there are political blogs, news blogs, blogs about a particular hobby, etc., etc.

Now, most blogs are not monologues, because they allow readers to make their own comments on what appears in the blog, or to add their own information to it. In this way, people get into contact with each other, learning from each other, sharing ideas, perhaps making friends or even doing business with each other, wherever they are in the world.

Although blogs are very much part of modern life and there are literally millions of blogs on the web, the history of blogging is a pretty short one. There is some disagreement over what the first blog was, but many people reckon it was an online diary started by a student called Justin Hall in 1994. His site was called *Justin's Home Page*, and he later called it *Links From The Underground*.

At that point, the word 'blog' didn't exist. More websites like his started to spring up, in the form of regularly updated online journals on various subjects, with links to other websites and forums for people to contribute their personal opinions.

In 1997, someone called Jorn Barger first used the term 'web log' to categorise this kind of website, when he launched his own website, *Robot Wisdom*. In 1999, a blogger called Peter Merholz jokingly broke this word up into 'we blog' and therefore invented the term 'blog'. Pretty soon, everyone called the sites 'blogs' and the people writing them 'bloggers'.

Pause

OK, now let's move on to how to run a blog, and what I'm going to do now is to tell you what I think is the best approach to workflow with a blog. First of all, you need to decide on the frequency of your blog posts. Some people do several a day, which is great if you can keep it up, others one a day. Once a week might be enough, but the key question is what the readers of your blog expect. They need to know when they can expect to see a new post on the blog, so whatever schedule you decide on, it's important to stick to it.

When you're going to do a post, start by reading material to find out what's being discussed in friends' blogs, or in other blogs related to the topic of yours. That way you can take these things into account to ensure that your blog is bang up to date.

Then start composing your blog post. If you're doing one that involves research and links, open a file for storing the sources of your information and the links you're going to put in the post. Also consider using pictures. These can make your blog much more attractive than one that's just text. If you use photos from the web, make sure you cite the source in your blog.

When you've completed the post, add some tags. If you don't have the kind of software that enables you to build them into the post, add them at the bottom. Tags are really important for searchability – they can get you new readers who find your blog via the tags.

If you think this is a particularly good post and you're really proud of it, announce it by sending links to it on social networking sites, together with a very brief summary of what it's about.

Then check your blog statistics to see how many people are reading and responding to your blog. Find out who's blogged about your post and reply to them, and give them a proper reply rather than just saying thanks.

After you've done all that, get off your own blog and comment elsewhere. Remember that you're not the only person blogging and putting out new material – there are lots of others doing the same and you should show them some respect by giving them comments and feedback on their posts where you feel it's appropriate.

Well, that's just some advice on being a good blogger. Blogging's obviously a major thing now in the world of electronic media and it's anybody's guess how it will develop in the future.

Unit 5

Track 6

You will hear a man who is interested in doing voluntary work connected with the environment talking to a woman who works for an organisation that runs environmental projects. First, you have some time to look at Questions 1–10.

Pause

Now listen and answer Questions 1–10.

Hannah   Hello, how can I help you?

Ryan   Well, I've come in because I want to volunteer for one of your environmental projects. I read something about your organisation in the paper a few days ago and I thought I'd like to get involved.

H   OK, that sounds good. What's your name?

R   Ryan.

H   OK, Ryan, thanks for coming in. I'm Hannah. Now, let me start by telling you something about our organisation and then we can have a look at a few projects that might interest you, after I've found out a bit about you.

R   Fine.

H   Right, well as you know, we're called *The Volunteer Agency* and that pretty well explains what we do. We recruit people for a wide range of projects. A lot of our work concerns environmental projects and at the moment we've got 130,000 volunteers working on these projects.

R   What sort of environmental projects are they?

H   Well, for example, if you wanted to go abroad, one of our big projects involves gathering information that is used for the protection of marine and forest environments. Volunteers on that do diving or collect biodiversity data on tropical rainforest species.

R   Sounds exciting. But I think I'd rather stay here, at least to start off with.

H   OK. Well, here in our own country we've got a big project aimed at clearing up litter in rural areas. The aim of this is to get everyone involved in making sure their local environment is clean and tidy.

R Yes, I've seen adverts for that.

H Another project involves looking after the National Cycle network, keeping the routes safe and attractive for cyclists. This is part of a bigger scheme concerned with developing sustainable transport systems all across the country.

R Interesting ...

H Now, if you want to do something in the city, rather than the countryside, within cities we also have the City Farms projects, which involve working with people, plants and animals.

R Oh, what are those? Are they real farms? How do they work?

H Well, yes, they're real farms and they're an example of a project that relies almost entirely on volunteers. On other projects, you might be working alongside salaried people, but with these, almost everyone is unpaid. In fact, many of our projects have very few, if any, paid staff.

R Yes, that's what I thought.

H Well, do any of these things sound particularly appealing to you?

R Well, as I say, I wasn't thinking of going abroad, and I'm not sure that any of those is exactly the sort of thing I'm really looking for. Sorry!

H That's OK, there are lots more things I can tell you about. I'm sure we'll find a project that's right up your street.

R Yes, I hope so.

H OK, well, let's have a look at a few other possibilities.

Pause

H Right, well one thing that might suit you is a scheme called *Wildlife Link*. There are 47 branches of this around the country, with over 24,000 active volunteers, and it's involved in all aspects of nature conservation. Its aim is to protect wildlife in all habitats across the country. Things you can do there include looking after nature reserves, taking part in community gardening and carrying out surveys of wildlife species. Tell me, are you keen to be outdoors?

R Yes, I am, and that does sound like the sort of thing I might be really interested in.

H OK. Well, here's another project that you might like the sound of. This one's aimed at young people.

R Right, tell me about that one.

H It's called *Wildlife Watch*, and involves organising groups for young people, getting them to explore and learn about their local environment. There are over 300 groups and around 150,000 members of those groups. As well as running those groups and going out with them, there is a need for volunteers with administrative skills. Is that the sort of thing you might fancy?

R Maybe, but I think I'd probably prefer to be more hands-on, doing physical work.

H OK. Well, then the organisation called *Action Earth* might be the one for you. They've got a total of 908 projects, involving over 18,000 volunteers. They do all sorts of things, from planting trees to constructing fences and walls and collecting litter, their aim being to improve the local environment in all sorts of ways. How does that sound?

R I might well be interested in that.

H OK, look, I'll give you some leaflets and contact information, and you can have a think about it all.

R That sounds like a good idea. Thanks.

Unit 6

Track 7

You will hear a manager in a museum talking to the staff about machines that are going to be put into the building. First, you have some time to look at Questions 1–10.

Pause

Now listen and answer Questions 1–10.

OK, now what we need to discuss next is vending machines. Now that the building has been completely refurbished, and we're going to be reopening, we should think of what kind of machines we need. These have two functions, of course – they provide services for visitors and they raise money. Every time someone buys something from the machine, we raise a little more money.

Well, first of all a cash machine seems like a good idea, so that people can get some money to spend while they're in the building, and this will help to keep down queues in the gift shop if everyone is paying with cards. That can go in the entrance hall – we thought about putting it in on the front wall outside the building but decided against that.

Now, we've also decided to install a ticket machine for the individual exhibitions in the various parts of the building. This will take some pressure off the ticket office and reduce the number of people hanging about in the entrance hall. It'll be a simple device – you select the exhibition and then pay for it in cash or by card and it'll be right next to the reception desk, with a sign above it so that people can clearly see it when they arrive.

Now the next machine lots of people might not approve of – a games machine for children to use. I know that this might not seem like the right sort of thing to have in a museum, but a constant complaint we get from visitors is that their visit is spoiled by the sound of bored children running around the corridors and shouting and generally disturbing the atmosphere. If we put a couple of these in the Visitor Centre, well away from the Exhibition Halls, it'll keep some of them occupied.

Then there's the question of a drinks machine. Well, we want as many people as possible to buy our own food and drink in the cafeteria and restaurant, but at the same time visitors will want something to drink when they're going round the museum and are not near to either of those places. We thought a good place for this would be by the lifts on the first floor as people go up and down from one exhibition to another and, of course, that's also right at the top of the stairs.

Pause

Now, the last thing is the drinks machine that we're putting in the staff room. As you'll be using this brand new state-of-the-art machine pretty frequently, I thought I'd just run through with you how it works. So, here on the screen I've put up a picture of it and I'll just tell you all how it works. Well, it's pretty big and you may be surprised to hear that it can store as many as 495 drinks products, so there'll be plenty to choose from and it won't need refilling too regularly.

Right, well, it's got a glass front here and behind it all the drinks, of course. The drinks come in bottles and cans and they're, of course, refrigerated. Now this machine has an interesting feature that I'm sure will entertain you all. When you've chosen and paid for your drink, there's a special rapid pick-up mechanism that grabs your drink and places it into the receiver, here, which is illuminated. So you can see your drink even if it's dark in here. And that's not all.

Through the glass front you can actually see the mechanism working – there's a visible moving arm that gets and delivers the drink and you can see that happening. Now, that's not just to make the machine interesting to look at while you're buying a drink, it's got a serious advantage too. What it does is to quickly and safely move the drink without it being shaken at all. So it won't bubble up or spill when you open it.

Now to the business of how you buy a drink. How it works is that you choose the drink you want from the menu here and then type in the code for that drink – you'll see the code in front of each drink. Then the price of the drink will be displayed here and you pay for it. You can do that with coins or by card. And you can order up to ten products at a time, for example, if you're getting drinks for a group of visitors or colleagues.

So, as I say, it's the very latest in drinks machine technology and I hope you'll all be pleased to have it.

Right, next I'm going to move on to talk about ...

Unit 7

Track 8

You will hear two students talking about a presentation that one of them is going to give. First, you have some time to look at Questions 1–10.

Pause

Now listen and answer Questions 1–10.

Jack   Hi Maya, how are you getting on with your presentation?

Maya   Oh, hi Jack. It's going really well after a slow start.

J   What's it about again?

M   Well, the general topic area is Human Relationships and we had to choose a specific area within that.

J   So, what have you chosen?

M   Lifelong Friendships.

J   Interesting. What led you to choose that?

M   Well, it occurred to me that there's been a lot of research on how people form friendships, and even more on marriage and partnerships, but there's not much on this particular topic. So, I thought I could do something a bit different by focusing on this particular aspect.

J   Sounds like a good idea. How have you been doing your research?

M   Well, mainly by personal contact. I realised that my parents have a number of lifelong friends, and of course, I've known them for years, so I thought I'd start off by seeing what they had to say.

J   Sounds reasonable, but that's only a very small sample, isn't it?

M   Yes, but I thought I'd collate the results from that small sample so that I could compare them with more general conclusions from research in the area.

J   Good idea. How did you get on when you tried to get information from your subjects?

M   Well, I started off by giving them a questionnaire. I spent quite some time working that out, deciding what aspects of their friendships I wanted them to focus on and then I handed it out to them.

J   And?

M   Well, it didn't work out too well. I kept asking for them back and they kept saying they hadn't had time to do them or hadn't quite finished them, and eventually one or two of them admitted that they were having trouble knowing what to put.

J   Oh, why's that?

M   They just couldn't analyse their friendships in that 'cold' way, on paper, in nice, neat little paragraphs or by ticking boxes. I realised then that they all felt that way, so I had to abandon that approach.

J   What did you do instead?

M   Personal interviews. I adapted my questionnaire and sat down with each person and talked to them. I got them to agree to my recording these interviews – that way I could focus on the way the interview went rather than having to write notes all the time – and then I went through the recordings.

J   And that worked out well?

M   Yes. I got all the information I needed. It was a small sample, as I say, but it was possible to get some general conclusions from them about their lifelong friendships.

J   And then you compared this with research data?

M   Yes, there's not a lot of that, but I managed to locate some academic research in the area.

J   And how did that compare with your findings?

M   Remarkably similar actually, so my sample proved to be pretty representative. There were one or two disparities here and there, but in general the research I was able to locate pretty much confirmed what I found myself.

Pause

J   Now, when you do your presentation, how have you organised it?

M   Well, obviously I've given that a lot of thought, and the various stages of the presentation are linked to the aspects I focused on when I was talking to my subjects. So, obviously, I start with how the friendship was first formed, for example, how old the people were, where they met, how they met, that kind of thing.

J   How will you present that?

M   I've created a table, with the various headings and the percentages of my subjects whose friendships started in the various ways.

J   OK, what comes next?

M   Well, I've looked at the effects on the friendship of various developments in the friends' lives. The first category I've called 'Change of Location', and that deals with what happens in the friendship if one or other of the friends goes to live somewhere else.

J   What about if they don't change the place where they live but go to work or study somewhere else?

M   Well, that's included in my data in that category, in a couple of separate tables.

J   What then?

M   OK, well then, I've looked at what happens to the friendship when one or both of the friends get married. I got the subjects to say simply whether marriage meant that friendships got less close, closer or stayed much the same.

J How have you presented that data?

M That's a pie chart.

J OK. What other aspects of the friendship have you focused on?

M Well, the next one concerns 'Personality'. I asked people to tick boxes for their friend's personality when they first met, and then how they would describe the same person now.

J How did you compare the answers there?

M Yea, that was tricky to work out. I looked for patterns of change. One finding from that was that many people who were described as 'relaxed' at the beginning of the friendship got categorised as 'stressed' right now. So, for the presentation, I picked out the most extreme changes that I found, not every single change.

J Sounds interesting. Any other categories?

M Yes, two more. I thought it would be interesting to compare how much people had in common in terms of political opinions as their friendship progressed over the years. Did they both change them, or did one person change and if so, did this cause tension or disagreement between them? I've constructed another pie chart for that.

J And the other category?

M Yes, I thought another key area concerned what the people have in common and whether they continue to have those things in common. I've categorised this as 'Shared Interests', and I've looked at any changes that tend to happen over the years. One thing I found, for example, was that men's shared passion for certain sports doesn't change at all over the years, whereas their musical tastes do.

J All sounds great. I'm sure it'll go well when you do the presentation.

M Thanks. I hope so.

Unit 8

Track 9

You will hear part of a lecture about the history of jeans. First, you have some time to look at Questions 1–10.

Pause

Now listen and answer Questions 1–10.

OK, today we're looking at contemporary fashion 'icons' as part of the module on the history and development of fashion. And perhaps the best place to start with this is with a garment that everybody in the world knows about and either wears or has worn – jeans.

Now, of course, jeans are often synonymous with the word 'denim', for the material they're made from. Where do both these terms come from? Well, there isn't universal agreement on either of these things, but the story begins in Europe in the 1500s. The general belief is that the word 'jeans' comes from Genoa in Italy, where sailors wore clothes made from a material called jean.

The word 'denim' is generally considered to come from France at roughly the same time. It is thought to have evolved from 'serge de Nîmes', a kind of material produced in the French town of Nîmes. These two fabrics were different in important ways. Denim was stronger and more expensive than jean. And denim was woven with one coloured thread and one white thread, while jean was woven with two coloured threads.

To start with, the cloth for both of them was a mixture of things. By the 18th century, however, it was made completely from cotton. And it was dark blue because it was dyed with indigo, which was taken from plants in the Americas and India. Denim and jean remained two very different fabrics and by the late 19th century it was denim that had emerged as the most popular and widely worn. Denim was used for workers' clothes, for example, those worn by workers on plantations, because it was very strong and it lasted for a long time. Jean was used for lighter clothes. Eventually of course, the word 'jeans' would come to be used for clothes made from denim, but that's much later.

A key event in the history of jeans was the 1848 Gold Rush, when gold was found in California and thousands of gold miners rushed there to find it and make their fortunes. They wanted clothes that were strong and didn't tear easily. Enter a man called Strauss. He moved to California from New York and started a business supplying work clothes. His first name was Leob, that's L-E-O-B. Later, he changed it to Levi.

Now, the miners in California were experiencing a problem with their work clothes. The pockets tore away from them very easily; they just weren't strong enough or well enough attached. In 1872, a man called Jacob Davis wrote to Strauss about an idea he'd had.

This was for metal rivets to hold the pockets and the rest of the garment together, and he offered Strauss a deal to use this idea in the clothes he was supplying. Strauss accepted the offer and started to make work clothes with these metal fasteners, made of copper. They weren't called jeans at this time, that term didn't come into being until the 1960s – they were sold as 'waist overalls' and made with denim.

In 1886, Strauss added another feature to these clothes, a leather label. To emphasize how strong the garments were, this showed a pair of these trousers being pulled between two horses. The message was that they were so strong that even this could not cause them to tear. By the 1920s, because of their reputation for toughness, Strauss's waist overalls were the most widely used workers' trousers in the U.S.

Now, up until the 1930s, jeans were purely and simply work clothes. But Hollywood changed all that and they made the journey to being fashion items. The roots of this lie in the cowboy movies of the 1930s. Cowboys often wore jeans in these movies, and American men wanted to dress like them in their free time. At this point, jeans are a wholly American thing.

The Second World War in the 1940s took them abroad, as American soldiers wore them when they were off duty. This introduced them to the wider world. But their real popularity as a fashion item really starts in the 1950s, when they caught on with young people. This was because they became the symbol of the teenage rebel. This completely new type of young person emerged in American films and TV programmes that were enormously popular with teenagers. Teenagers didn't call the clothes 'waist overalls', they gave them a new name – 'jean pants'. And pretty soon, this got abbreviated to jeans.

In the 1960s, jeans were the standard kind of trousers worn by students in Western countries and they were the top fashion item. Young people adapted them in all sorts of ways, turning them into embroidered jeans by sewing brightly coloured designs on to them, and all sorts of styles emerged, one of the main ones being flared jeans, with bottoms that got wider and wider as they went down.

Right, now I'm going to move on to look at what jeans symbolised both in Western countries and in non-Western countries at that time. But first of all, does anyone have any questions?

Acknowledgements

Development of this publication has made use of the Cambridge International Corpus (CIC). The CIC is a computerised database of contemporary spoken and written English which currently stands at over one billion words. It includes British English, American English and other varieties of English. It also includes the Cambridge Learner Corpus, developed in collaboration with the University of Cambridge ESOL Examinations. Cambridge University Press has built up the CIC to provide evidence about language use that helps to produce better language teaching materials.

The authors and publishers acknowledge the following sources of copyright material and are grateful for the permissions granted. While every effort has been made, it has not always been possible to identify the sources of all the material used, or to trace all copyright holders. If any omissions are brought to our notice, we will be happy to include the appropriate acknowledgements on reprinting.

Text

Telegraph Media Group Limited for the text on p. 8 'Third Culture Kids' from 'Third Culture Kids' by Ruth E Van Reken, *The Telegraph*, 13.11.09, for the text on pp. 12–13 'What do you know about the food you eat?' adapted from 'Food Science and food myths: Bond may have been onto something' by Mick O'Hare, *The Telegraph*, 5.10.10,
pp. 20–21 'Strictly English' adapted from 'Simon Heffer: The Corrections' by Simon Heffer, *The Telegraph*, 20.8.10 and 'Strictly English: Part Two' by Simon Heffer, *The Telegraph*, 27.8.10, pp. 24–25 'Is constant use of electronic media changing our minds?' from 'Are Twitter and Facebook affecting how we think?' by Neil Tweedie, The Telegraph, 28.6.10, pp. 32–33 'Russia's boreal forests and wild grasses could combat climate change' from 'Russia's boreal forests may help to combat climate change' by Kristofar Ivanovich, *The Telegraph*, 29.4.10, pp. 36–37 'Movers and Shakers' from 'Clothes retailer White Stuff listens to the customer' by Helen Dunne, *The Telegraph* 27.1.09 and 'HomePride MD proud to see oven cleaning kits rack up fine profits' by Helen Dunne, *The Telegraph*, 9.6.09, p. 44 'Establishing your birthrights' from 'Establishing your birthrights' by Clover Stroud, *The Telegraph Weekend*, 16.1.10, pp. 48–49 'Making a loss is the height of fashion' from 'Haute couture: Making a loss is the height of fashion' by William Langley, *The Sunday Telegraph*, 11.7.10. Copyright © Telegraph Media Group Limited;

European Foundation for the Improvement of Living and Working Conditions for the two graphs on p.10 adapted from the European Working Conditions Observatory (http://www.eurofound.europa.eu/ewco). Reproduced by permission;

Paul H Brookes Publishing Co Inc., for the charts on p. 21 adapted from *Meaningful Differences in the Everyday Experience of Young Children* written by Hart & Risley.

Copyright © 1995, Paul H Brookes Publishing Co., Inc, Baltimore. Adapted by permission;

Futurelab Education for the table on p. 23 adapted from 'Which communication skills are essential in your job?' Survey 1997 and 2006 http://www.beyondcurrenthorizons.org.uk/. Reproduced with permission;

Osaka Gas Group for the diagram on p. 34 from the *Osaka Gas Group CSR Report 2009*. Reproduced with permission;

Diagram on p. 35 from The Energy Star Program (www.energystar.gov);

Your Workplace for the pie charts on p. 46 originally published in the July/August 2009, volume 11-4, issue of *Your Workplace magazine, Live Healthy. Work Smart.* Reprinted with permission. www.yourworkplace.ca

Photos

Key: TL = top left TR = top right

p. 8: Thinkstock; p. 16 (TR): Thinkstock/Comstock; p. 16 (TL) and 17: Shutterstock/Monkey Business Images; p. 19: iStock/© Jennifer Sharp; p. 24: Thinkstock/Jupiterimages; p. 27: Thinkstock/Stockbyte; p. 29: Thinkstock/Goodshoot; p. 32: Shutterstock/shalunishka; p. 37 (TR): ©Phil Weedon/White Stuff/www.prshots.com; p. 37 (TL): Photograph of Terence Leahy from Newscast; p. 39: Getty Images/Eric Audras/ONOKY; p. 40: Thinkstock; p. 44: Thinkstock/Jack Hollingsworth; pp. 48–49: © Getty Images/Antonio de Moraes Barros Filho/WireImage; p. 50: Shutterstock/crystalfoto; p. 53: Thinkstock/Brand X Pictures.

Commissioned photo on p. 20: Sophie Clarke/Cambridge University Press

Illustrations

Kveta pp. 6, 12, 18, 28, 30, 39, 41, 42, 47, 52; Peter Marriage pp. 10, 14, 22, 23, 45, 46; Andrew Painter pp. 35, 37; Martin Saunders pp. 34; David Whamond p. 11; Gary Wing pp. 7, 26

The publishers are grateful to the following contributors:

Judith Greet: editorial work

Kevin Doherty: proofreader

John Green: audio producer

Tim Woolf: audio editor

Cover design and page layout: Wild Apple Design Ltd

Audio recorded at: I.D. Audio Studios, London